GET
GROWING

GET GROWING

Keys to Unlocking the Potential of Your Small Business

DAVID WILTON & KYLE McNAMARA

KEY PORTER BOOKS

Library and Archives Canada Cataloguing in Publication

Wilton, David, 1956-
    Get growing : keys to unlocking the potential in your small business / David
Wilton, Kyle McNamara.

ISBN 978-1-55470-195-7

    1. Small business--Growth. 2. Entrepreneurship. 3. Business planning.
4. Success in business. 5. Success in business--Canada--Case studies.
I. McNamara, Kyle, 1970- II. Title.

HD62.7.W573 2009   658.4'06   C2009-901833-0

ONTARIO ARTS COUNCIL
CONSEIL DES ARTS DE L'ONTARIO

The publisher gratefully acknowledges the support of the Canada Council for the
Arts and the Ontario Arts Council for its publishing program. We acknowledge the
support of the Government of Ontario through the Ontario Media Development
Corporation's Ontario Book Initiative.

We acknowledge the financial support of the Government of Canada through the Book
Publishing Industry Development Program (BPIDP) for our publishing activities.

® Registered trademarks of the Bank of Nova Scotia.
™ Trademarks of the Bank of Nova Scotia
®* Intuit and the Intuit logo are trademarks of Intuit Canada Limited or one of its
affiliates registered in Canada and other countries.

Key Porter Books Limited
Six Adelaide Street East, Tenth Floor
Toronto, Ontario
Canada M5C 1H6

Mixed Sources
Product group from well-managed
forests, controlled sources and
recycled wood or fiber
www.fsc.org Cert no. SW-COC-002358
© 1996 Forest Stewardship Council
FSC

ANCIENT FOREST™
FRIENDLY

www.keyporter.com

Printed and bound in Canada

09 10 11 12 13 5 4 3 2 1

CONTENTS

INTRODUCTION

From Victoria, British Columbia, to St. John's, Newfoundland, small business owners are a driving force powering the Canadian economy. Every day, in communities large and small, they strive to harness the potential of their enterprises. They provide a wide array of products and services, and are continually adapting and innovating, responding effectively to changing market conditions. In the process, they are creating more than 60 per cent of the total employment in this country.

These business owners are living out their dreams. They are contributing to strong communities, living fulfilling lifestyles, and often achieving the financial independence they've long sought. They are a vibrant part of the fabric of Canada, making our collective lives richer.

THE GET GROWING *FOR BUSINESS* TOUR

In the summer of 2008, we had a unique opportunity to better understand the broad scope of expertise and experience that resides with Canadian small business owners.

We packed up a thirty-eight-foot RV and set out on what we called our "Get Growing *for business* Tour." Over the course of five months, we travelled from the west coast of Canada all the way across to the Maritimes. Along the way we met with hundreds of small business owners and experienced the collective wisdom they had gained in the school of hard knocks.

In total we stopped in more than eighty communities to meet with a wide variety of entrepreneurs, visiting their places of business, and inviting them to join us in the RV we called home. We listened to their ideas as well as their perspectives on what worked well for them and what worked, as one business owner said, "not so much!"

After a while we were hearing common themes from many of the business owners we spoke to. On the one hand, they loved owning their own business. Most were incredibly passionate about the product or service that originally drew them into the venture in the first place, and if you asked them if they would ever work for anyone else again, their answer was a resounding "No!" At the same time, however, they had to overcome the reality of dealing with the diverse requirements of running a business. The demands on their time included managing their sales and marketing programs, their financial position, their human resources, and their operations. This often bogged them down and made it difficult to achieve the potential they knew existed within their business. Still, time after time, we heard success stories from entrepreneurs who had met these challenges—and had overcome them.

Business owners highlighted that each business is a work in progress. It reveals the sum total of the challenges and opportunities it has faced over time. The business reflects the successes and failures of each owner to make the right day-to-day choices required to manage both the critical as well as the mundane aspects of running a business. These are important decisions, many of which are key to achieving the owner's long-term business goals.

The concept for the book took shape as we recognized the potential of the information we gathered from people we met on our cross-Canada journey. We began to explore the idea that:

- Small business owners oversee complex businesses that require expertise in a wide range of management areas, including sales, marketing, finance, risk management, and much, much more. Needless to say, it's a difficult job!

- When viewed as a group, Canadian small businesses have both the expertise and the experience to deal with all aspects of business management—and to do so successfully. Different business owners bring different sets of knowledge and capabilities to their enterprises. Collectively, their understanding of what it takes to be successful in the real world is indisputable.

- By tapping into the combined wisdom of this larger collective group of small business owners, it becomes possible to link individual entrepreneurs to a vast wealth of resources and perspectives. These resources and perspectives can help entrepreneurs make decisions that will unlock the growth potential in their small businesses.

In this book, we capture the knowledge that has made Canadian entrepreneurs successful. Chapter by chapter, you will meet many of the small business owners we encountered during our 2008 tour. We'll zero in on some of the perspectives and strategies that have worked for each of them. At the same time, we will focus on some basic and not-so-basic approaches that can help you chart a course to increase success in your business.

Clearly there is no magic formula in small business. The small business marketplace in Canada is extremely varied. It contains retailers, health-care professionals, agricultural industries, professional service firms, manufacturers, skilled trades, and so on. These businesses sell directly to consumers, to government, and to other businesses large and small. It's unrealistic to think the exact same strategies that work for one will work for another. However, there are some general characteristics of flourishing businesses. We have leveraged these characteristics, as well as the stories of small business owners we met, to create "unlocking keys." These are guiding principles you can capitalize on to make your business even more successful.

TWO COMMON THEMES IN SUCCESSFUL SMALL BUSINESSES

There were two overarching principles we observed in many successful businesses. First, we would regularly find ourselves discussing the role of a business plan in guiding the decisions and strategies of business owners. Second, we would hear how the business owner had benefitted from the input of advisers. Most notably, these conversations tended to occur in businesses that were thriving.

We made the connection.

In fact, these two themes reoccurred so frequently in successful businesses that they warrant special emphasis early in this book.

Successful Business Owners:
1. Construct a written business plan to guide them.
2. Surround themselves with the right team of advisers.

We'll present these two principles as the first of many unlocking keys you'll find throughout this book. Our purpose is to highlight those practices that were most often mentioned as being critical for any business targeting growth. Many of the unlocking keys will be linked to more detailed worksheets or tools designed to help you consider how you might apply each unlocking key to your business. We've highlighted these as "Online Resources" throughout the book. We encourage you to visit the website **www.getgrowingforbusiness.com/ unlocking** to access these complementary resources and further explore how you can translate the ideas you discover in this book into practical, actionable steps that you can use in your business.

Writing Business Plans

UNLOCKING KEY: The construction of a written business plan creates a roadmap to success.

Many entrepreneurs identified a business plan as the cornerstone of their businesses. It became a guide for them and all their stakeholders, including employees, investors, suppliers, and advisers.

There is no need to be intimidated by the thought of constructing a business plan. It doesn't need to be long—just straightforward and concise. When business owners showed us their business plans, they typically included the following elements:

Executive Summary

The executive summary concisely highlights the information and insights found within the business plan.

Business Description

This section of the business plan contains information about the business, including a background on how the enterprise came about and what it has achieved, a definition of what's important to the business, and a short description of the products or services it provides. The business description also establishes specific milestones for measuring success in the future.

Marketplace

The marketplace section explains how the business is positioned in a larger context. It identifies and examines the competition and describes the types of customers that the business actively targets.

Sales and Marketing
Very simply, this portion of the business plan focuses on the business's strategy for attracting new customers and keeping its existing customer base.

Business Operations
The business operations section answers questions such as How does the business work? Who are its suppliers? What level of staffing is required?

Financial Information
Finally, this section provides the financial skeleton of the business, including historical results, the current balance sheet showing what the company owns and what it owes, as well as projected balance sheets, income statements, and cash-flow projections that will reflect the growth of the business over time. It's also important to include personal financial statements for the owners of the business to demonstrate their ability to contribute to the business.

> **Get Growing *for business* Online Resource:** Scotia Plan Writer *for business*™ is a comprehensive, interactive business plan writer you can use to create a customized plan for your business (**www.getgrowingforbusiness. com/mytools**).

Why is a business plan so critical for success? It allows the business to:

- stay focused on the business owner's goals and vision. It also helps align all the business's stakeholders and advisers around the business's goals.
- forecast and anticipate problems—whether financial or within other essential aspects of the business, like inventory supply or threats to the customer base.
- leverage the business owner's strengths and mitigate weaknesses. Business owners can't be experts in all areas. The business plan provides a framework to consider these strengths and weaknesses and define strategies accordingly.
- become the framework for conversations with potential lenders, investors, key employees, suppliers, and sometimes even customers.
- measure the business's progress and plans for the future. The plan defines success as well as key shorter-term milestones. These can be measured and adjusted as the plan evolves.

Business owners who had created business plans highlighted that planning is not static—it is very much a process. The planning process goes through the following steps:

1. You identify a key business issue or opportunity.
2. You consider alternatives and weigh the pros and cons of each.
3. You choose what you deem to be the best alternative for your situation.
4. You execute the chosen strategy.
5. You measure the outcome.

The alternatives and strategies you consider will require you to make assumptions. It's important to use your business plan to test these assumptions. For example, if you import or export to the United States, you need to assess the impact of changes in the exchange rate on your business's financial position. Use your financial projections to test a few "what if" scenarios based on different assumptions about what exchange rates might be. Examine their bottom-line impact and anticipate any related issues that may become evident such as additional capital or staff requirements.

Then, depending on the nature of the outcome, you may feel that it worked well for your particular business issue, or you may want to consider another one of the alternatives.

In uncertain times, it is especially worthwhile to regularly review and update your business plan to help you mitigate business or financial challenges. Things change and you need to stay one step ahead. You may want to assess the potential impact of a drop in revenue or an increase in costs, and to define appropriate business strategies accordingly. If unforeseen events drive this outcome, you want to be prepared to respond. We'll talk more about mitigating business risks in Chapter 7.

Working with Advisers

UNLOCKING KEY: Surrounding yourself with the right team of advisers will assist you with working "on" the business instead of always "in" the business.

Business owners are often required to wear a variety of hats, simultaneously acting in the roles of chief executive officer, chief operating officer, chief financial officer, head of sales and marketing, head of human resources, head of information technology, and so on. Clearly, this is a challenge.

Surrounding yourself with the right advisers will help you become more strategic in your approach to your business. We met a number of small business owners who were able to grow their business to the next level only after their advisers encouraged them to take a step back and look at the big picture.

These entrepreneurs had been preoccupied with the important day-to-day operations of the business. They were doing the activities they loved. Their advisers challenged them to consider where they wanted to bring their business next and to define their priorities by identifying major personal and business goals. These same advisers then helped them define the action plans that would allow the business owners to get there.

Small business owners are incredibly passionate about their business. They need to be. As a small business owner, you have no doubt encountered a dizzying range of highs and lows. Through it all, your passion and commitment keep you focused. Sometimes, though, this passion convinces small business owners to create overly optimistic assumptions.

Good advisers challenge your assumptions. They highlight potential risks in your business plan and encourage you to consider different viewpoints and alternative strategies. They have a great deal of experience working with other small business owners and can help translate successful strategies they have seen before into tangible recommendations for you.

Your team of advisers will likely include an accountant or bookkeeper, a lawyer, a small business banker, as well as a coach or mentor experienced in your industry.

A World of Advisers

The small business owners that we met referred to a wide range of advisers who helped them in their business ventures, including:

- accountants
- bankers
- coaches
- family
- friends
- lawyers
- librarians
- mentors
- other small business owners
- parents
- teachers

Exploring Growth in All Businesses

This book is primarily designed for established businesses. It highlights strategies to help them achieve the level of success that they want to attain—no matter how this "success" is defined.

However, the book also provides a roadmap for new business start-ups. New business owners will learn that the challenges and opportunities they will soon encounter have already been met by their peers in other businesses. We will highlight those profitable tactics that enhance strengths and diminish weaknesses, as well as best practices to accelerate success, so that new business owners can factor them directly into their business plans.

Ultimately, this book is about linking all business owners to the possibility of leveraging the combined wisdom of small businesses from across the country. This achievement is attained not only through the suggestions and practices contained within the pages of this book, but also by offering a way to actively and directly interact with other small business owners through the online small business community at **www.getgrowingforbusiness.com/unlocking**. It's all about taking your planning to the next level, getting access to new resources, and connecting with advisers and other small business owners who can help you explore your growth possibilities.

It is our hope that you will benefit from this collective wisdom and unlock growth in ways that you may never have expected.

1

SETTING PERSONAL AND BUSINESS GOALS

Center City Tire & Auto

Jeff Roberts's first venture in the auto repair business was in 1994, from a single bay in the back of a building in Red Deer, Alberta. Within two years he was transforming his business, moving into a gas station with a convenience store and several bays, and carrying a small staff. In 2000, he refined his business with a stronger focus on service ("We're in the knowledge business," he says), moving into Center City Tire & Auto's current location in Red Deer. In 2004, he purchased a second business—an existing venture that was losing money—and doubled its sales. In 2006, Center City expanded—doubling in size to 10,000 square feet. Continuing his growth strategy, Jeff opened his third auto service business in Innisfail, Alberta, in 2008.

Along the way, Jeff used his strong people skills to help his customers, and to hire and retain qualified and knowledgeable staff. He used his business skills to grow his small operation from the back of a building into three strong businesses. He has also been able to support his community, particularly the children who live there, through local lacrosse and hockey teams, as well as youth anti-bullying programs.

It is not surprising to hear that Jeff's business success is a natural outcome of his personal goal to strive to be better every day. His advice to other business owners is, "Focus on today and what you're going to do. Know that every day you're going to make a mistake. What's important is to learn from that mistake and improve yourself." Visit the company's website at **www.wrenchmasters.com**.

When it comes right down to it, you likely started your business to help you achieve your personal goals.

These goals reflect what's important to you. Personal goals may be financial in nature, such as to become financially independent, or they may be tied to a sense of social responsibility, such as improving our environment. Or you may have lifestyle goals that you hope to achieve as a result of owning a business, such as flexible working hours.

To identify your goals, you simply need to ask yourself how you measure personal success. Is it by achieving financial goals, contributing to the broader community, or some other measure that's important to you? You may find you have multiple goals or perhaps you will discover that your goals evolve as your circumstances change over time. For example, flexible hours may be important while your children are in school, and a full-time commitment may become more practical as they get older.

It's important to identify your personal priorities and to restate or redefine your goals on a regular basis.

UNLOCKING KEY: The first step in building a plan for business success is to define what personal success is.

How you define personal success will help you define business success. If your personal goals are largely financial in nature, the same will be true of your business goals. Similarly, if your personal goals are lifestyle oriented, then your business goals will be too. As an example, consider a cyclist who began her business of training other cyclists to promote the sport. The primary goals for this business are not financial in nature. Success is not defined in terms of net income or revenue growth. Instead, it's based on the students being trained, and the success that they achieve. Defining your personal goals helps you identify what you want to get out of owning a business and will better enable you to achieve personal fulfillment as business goals align to personal ones.

> Get Growing *for business* Online Resource: The Personal Goal Identification worksheet helps you identify your personal priorities and document your key personal goals (www.getgrowingforbusiness.com/unlocking/goals).

UNLOCKING YOUR BUSINESS GOALS

Once you have identified your personal goals, it becomes easier to define goals for your business. Small business owners across the country define success in different ways, but when we asked them to highlight their key business goals, they were often financial. In a comprehensive research survey we conducted in 2007, increasing operating income or profit margin was cited as a key business goal by 89 per cent of respondents. This was followed by generating double-digit growth, cited by 65 per cent of respondents.

> **Top Financial Goals of Canadian Businesses**
> - Increasing operating income or profit margin: 89 per cent
> - Generating double-digit growth: 65 per cent
> - Reducing cost structure: 60 per cent
> - Improving administrative practices: 59 per cent

UNLOCKING KEY: Identify your key business goals.

Businesses with a clear picture of what they are striving to accomplish look and feel different than businesses that do not have clear goals. Businesses with a plan are focused, directing their energy to clearly defined objectives. Clear goals help them choose one option over another, making more targeted decisions—like a contractor who had decided to increase margins by making it his goal to be the recognized expert in energy-efficient construction technology in his market area, or a café owner who made it her goal to focus on making delicious organic baked goods a new option for the lunch crowd in her city.

Goals versus Strategies

By identifying clear goals for your business you will find it easier to choose strategies to achieve those goals. It's important to understand the difference between a goal and a strategy. A goal is the outcome you hope to achieve. A strategy is the action you will take to achieve the goal. Say you want to increase sales in your retail store. This is your goal. The possible strategies you could use to achieve this goal might be to increase foot traffic by offering a sale, or advertise a new product, for example.

Targeting Your Goals

So, what are your key business goals? Are they financial or non-financial? Be honest with yourself about what you want, and continue to ask yourself questions to make your goals as specific as possible.

If your goals are indeed financial, focus on precisely what you want to achieve. Is it double-digit growth? If so, what is your target growth rate (i.e., 25 per cent)? Is it to improve cash flow by, say, $10,000 or reduce costs by $1,000 a month, for example? Do you have targets in mind?

Are you targeting improved bottom-line profitability? How many dollars of profit will you achieve? Is that before or after tax?

Do you have operational goals, such as expanding your business premises or increasing the number of employees?

If your goals are not financial, what do they centre on? Is

your goal to create a business to pass on to your children? Do you want to improve your community in general, or meet the needs of a specific segment of your community, such as children or the elderly?

Whatever the Goal, Write It Down, and Make It SMART:

- **Specific:** Ensure your goal is clearly defined and identified.
- **Measurable:** Pinpoint a specifically measured outcome, like reaching 50,000 people or doubling your profits.
- **Achievable:** Goals must be achievable through specific actions.
- **Realistic:** Ensure that the precise expectations of the goal are practical, and a good fit for you and your life.
- **Timetabled:** Put a time limit on achieving your goal; for example, in a month, a year, or by next quarter.

It's worth pointing out that you may have more than one key business goal. On the other hand, avoid the pitfall of having too many goals. More than two or three simply become unmanageable, making it more difficult to choose when goals have competing priorities.

Protocase

Steve Lilley and Doug Milburn started Protocase in Sydney, Nova Scotia, in 2001. The company sells custom metal electronic enclosures to a customer base made up mostly of designers and engineers. Customers can send in their designs using their own design software or the software that Protocase has available on its website.

The company's competitive advantage is significant. Protocase offers a combination of speed with the potential for low-volume orders. Customers can order their custom-designed enclosures in small quantities—right down to a single prototype—and will receive their order in just a few days.

Protocase's customers are excited to see something that they've designed on a computer turned into a tangible product—and so quickly.

"It's all about the customer," says Doug. "Make them happy, deliver an experience to them, and you'll prosper." Visit the company's website at **www.protocase.com**.

COMPETITIVE ADVANTAGE

UNLOCKING KEY: Defining your business model and your competitive advantage will help you achieve the key goals of your business.

What is it that makes your business successful? Why do customers choose to do business with you rather than someone else? Why do repeat customers keep coming back?

This is your competitive advantage. It is something you do or something you have that customers prefer. It's a relative position you hold in the marketplace. As such, to help define your competitive advantage, inventory the competition in your marketplace and consider the industry you operate within.

Business owners gave us some examples of various sources of competitive advantage:

- **Expertise:** Your business provides a level of knowledge or technical skills customers prefer.
- **Service:** Pre- or after-sale service is exceptional. Customers want the extra focus on them and their needs.
- **Convenience:** The physical and/or electronic accessibility of your business sets you apart.
- **Price:** Your price point (potentially in combination with other attributes such as service or convenience) is extraordinary.
- **Quality:** Certain features of your product or service are better aligned to meet customer needs.
- **Uniqueness:** The features or combination of features of your product or service are uncommon.
- **Speed:** You can develop or deliver your products or your service faster.
- **Combination:** Any combination of the above can be merged.

Be sure to strengthen and protect this competitive advantage. How can you do this? The best way is to define the tactics that reinforce the unique position you hold in the marketplace. For example, if your competitive advantage is expertise, you may introduce an extensive training program that builds staff knowledge of your product or service.

Get Growing *for business* Online Resource: The Business Goal and Competitive Advantage worksheets help you pinpoint your key business goals, and then identify aspects of your business that deliver a competitive advantage (www.getgrowingforbusiness.com/unlocking/goals).

It's a powerful combination when an entrepreneur's personal goals are extended to relevant business goals, and are finally transformed into a business model that creates an enterprise with a unique competitive advantage. With these building blocks in place, the task of finding the right strategies to optimize the results of the business becomes much easier, but still requires very deliberate planning and implementation.

UNLOCKING KEY: Identify strategy alternatives before choosing the activities you will need to undertake to reach your particular business goals.

BRAINSTORMING

Once you identify your goals and competitive advantages, your next step is to develop a list of strategies you might use to achieve them. It comes down to creating an inventory of strategy options—alternatives you could implement to deliver the results you're looking for. Initially, it amounts to a process of brainstorming.

Part of the challenge is to move beyond your own frame of reference to generate some new ideas you have not previously considered. This book is designed to help you do exactly that. Consider the experience of those businesses we have highlighted on these pages. Also be sure to log on to **www.getgrowingforbusiness.com/unlocking** to take part in online discussions, and connect with other small business owners who may be able to identify approaches that have worked for them.

This is another benefit of a strong team of advisers. Many business owners highlight the importance of leveraging your advisers as a source of new ideas.

Understand that while your independent streak may help sustain your drive and enthusiasm, it may also have the un-intended consequence of isolating you by predisposing you to work alone. In isolation, it is much more difficult to benefit from the advice and perspective of others. Other people's experiences are the very things that can help you identify options and alternatives that could fast-track your strategies and help you achieve your goals. So be deliberate, network with other business owners, and read this book and the success stories within. Sign onto the website and connect to the broader online small business community. Most of all, remain open to new ideas that can help you identify new alternatives.

Ideally, you will want to identify potential strategies by:

- devoting time to researching your alternatives;
- gathering information from others who have been suc-cessful in achieving similar goals;
- drawing from your personal experiences; and
- thinking creatively, considering ideas that may initially seem impractical.

Remember, at this early stage, the goal is to generate a large quantity of ideas, as opposed to focusing on quality.

For example, let's consider a home landscaping business. Let's assume the business has adopted the goal of generating double-digit growth in the next fiscal year. The owners need to consider strategy alternatives to achieve this goal. Initially, they need to contemplate sales and marketing strategies. A brainstorming session may produce alternatives such as:

- expanding their sales force;
- dropping leaflets in targeted neighbourhoods;
- creating awareness by offering to write a column in the local paper's home section;
- contacting past and existing customers and requesting customer referrals;
- participating in trade shows, home shows, or other industry events;
- building awareness and local media coverage of their business by donating labour to revitalize the landscape of a local organization such as a school;
- partnering with interior home designers or some other non-competitive business to co-promote each other; and
- building an online catalogue of customer testimonials and successful jobs.

Most of us are wired to short-circuit this process of generating an inventory of alternatives to choose from, especially when we're consumed with the day-to-day operations of running a small business. For many the tendency is to:

- devote little time to generating alternatives;
- skip the process of gathering opinions from others; and
- go with the first strategy considered.

Resist the temptation to reject ideas as you come up with them. Capture them on paper first—no matter how unrealistic, outlandish, or silly they may seem. Truly consider how each could be successful rather than concentrating on why none of them will work.

With your list of strategy alternatives in hand, pick those approaches you believe have the greatest likelihood of achieving the goals you have established for your business. You will also want to ensure that these strategies will further your desired competitive advantage.

Consider creating a list of criteria to judge each of your options. Then score the strategy alternatives against the criteria. Assign higher scores to those options you believe will most likely help you achieve your goals. From a practical perspective, you'll also need to consider if your business has or could acquire the necessary resources to pursue the strategy alternative. Your criteria will be unique to your business situation, but here are some ideas to get you started.

Rank each alternative from 1 to 10, asking yourself if the strategy alternative:

- has been proven successful by others who have tried it;
- can be undertaken with the team you have;
- can be undertaken with the financial resources you have available;
- can be undertaken with the time you have available;
- will further develop your competitive advantage; and
- has a high likelihood of achieving your goal.

Once you score each of your alternatives, pick the highest-ranking two or three alternatives as your top candidates. Now investigate these more fully. Research the pros and cons of each approach in detail. Determine if there are any unintended consequences and, if so, steps you can take to mitigate their effect. Consider not only the degree to which the strategy may contribute to your top-line goal, but be sure to look deeper at the broader effects on other aspects of your business. Talk to peers and advisers about your intended approach. Listen carefully to their advice. Think through the practical steps of implementing the strategies. Consider again the timelines, skills, and abilities of your team, and the financial resources you have available. Throughout the entire process, try to keep an open mind as you assess each idea.

It is also important to consider the financial impact of each strategy. Pull out your business plan and plug in the numbers on both the cash-flow projection and your pro forma income and balance sheets.

Now sit back and consider the alternatives for a day or two. Evaluate the information you have gathered. A healthy dose of realism is important as you make your choice, picking the strategy alternative with the best fit and the one most likely to achieve your intended goal.

UNLOCKING KEY: Choose a strategy that is realistic for your business and has the highest likelihood of achieving your intended goal.

Get Growing *for business* Online Resource: The Strategy Alternative worksheet provides a framework that will lead you through a process for brainstorming strategy alternatives. Evaluating those alternatives by assessing their potential to deliver outcomes that will achieve your identified goals. Choosing the option with the highest potential for success (**www.getgrowingforbusiness.com/unlocking/goals**).

IMPLEMENTING YOUR STRATEGY

With the strategy decision made, you will need to map out a plan to implement your chosen approach. While your approach will vary depending on the scope of the strategy, it should be carefully documented, with an action plan clearly establishing who does what and when, and how you will monitor results.

Here is a framework to help you work through the various aspects of implementing a chosen strategy.

Strategy Description
Concisely describe the strategy you have chosen.

Strategy Objectives
Define the specific outcomes you expect your strategy to deliver, relating them back to your key business goal.

Process Construction
Most strategies will require the creation of new processes within your business or the reconstruction of old ones. Whether you are implementing new cost-control mechanisms or undertaking a new marketing program, a new strategy will need to be supported by internal (or perhaps even external) processes to ensure the initiative is fully integrated into existing business practices. Think through the existing process changes that will be required, and document each one.

Implementation Plans
Outline the specific action items necessary to implement each new process. For each separate process, identify what the

change is, then create specific tasks to implement the change. Be sure to include not only what each step is, but also who has responsibility for it and when each is to be completed.

Communication

Consider who will be affected by the changes and be sure to communicate ahead of time to those people, including your staff, customers, or suppliers. Consider involving key employees in the process of creating the new processes and developing the new action plans. By involving some of those individuals who would be affected, you can increase their commitment to the new initiative.

Monitor Results

As you create the process, be clear about the intended outcomes and devise mechanisms by which to measure your results. This could include financial benchmarks, customer satisfaction surveys, or traffic counts—whatever you can use to evaluate the success of the strategy.

UNLOCKING KEY: Create a detailed plan outlining how you will implement your chosen strategy, who does what and by when, and specific measures that will allow you to monitor the success of the initiative.

Get Growing *for business* Online Resource: The Strategy Implementation worksheet provides a framework that can help you create a process to implement the strategies you have chosen (**www.getgrowingforbusiness.com/ unlocking/goals**).

J&L PowerSports

Jeffrey Norman started J&L PowerSports in 2008 in Cornwall, Ontario. As a motocross enthusiast, he felt there was a serious lack of attention to detail and variety in power sports through-out the area and decided to assess the market. He took his time and put together a detailed business plan. "It's my roadmap for the business," he says.

In less than a year, he has surpassed his three-year projections.

"A business plan is a testament to what you believe," says Jeff. He continues to look at his plan regularly to keep his business focused. That's why if a customer asks him if he plans to start carrying products like skis or snowshoes, he quickly centres on the fact that his niche is as a power-sports business, and not a general outdoors retailer.

"It's important to devote your time to boundaries and stay within them," he says. Visit the company's website at **www.jlpowersports.com**.

A FEW WORDS FOR START-UPS

Understanding personal goals, translating them into business goals, and identifying your competitive advantage is important for entrepreneurs who are starting new businesses. New entrepreneurs have to deal with the reality that practical perspectives come from experience. You may have heard the old saying: "You do not know what you do not know." When you combine your lack of experience with the natural enthusiasm of pursuing an exciting new idea, you run the risk of setting unrealistic goals.

Be encouraged by reading this book and others like it. You can begin to benefit from the experience of others and to some degree incorporate it as your own. Don't lose your enthusiasm! It will power you through the inevitable ups and downs of a start-up. But temper your enthusiasm with a willingness to be influenced by others. Read, talk to other entrepreneurs, find advisers you can rely on, go online, and learn, learn, learn. The time you invest now will help you to better understand the issues you will be facing and help you anticipate appropriate strategies and solutions, while avoiding potential pitfalls.

2

SALES AND MARKETING STRATEGIES

Black Fly Beverage Company Inc.

Rob Kelly and Cathy Siskind-Kelly founded this micro-distillery in London, Ontario, in May 2005. They tapped into the ready-to-drink beverage market at a critical time and offer a unique vodka-based product line with a bold taste, which contains natural fruit juices, without the usual sweetness.

Since its inception, Black Fly Coolers has expanded beyond its original Ontario market, where it's carried by 83 per cent of LCBO stores, into Nova Scotia, Alberta, British Columbia, and Yukon.

The CBC profiled Black Fly's start-up on the TV show *Venture*. When it comes to the company's sales and marketing strategy, "We don't do straight, paid advertising," says Cathy. They are more likely to call up a magazine and say, "We have a story for you." The company also maintains an attractive website.

"Our favourite way to spend money is for people to try the product," says Cathy. They offer tastings at LCBO outlets, sporting events, festivals, and concerts. "From there, the word of mouth grows," she says. Visit the company's website at **www.blackflycoolers.com**.

Every small business generates income by delivering products or services to people who are willing to pay for them—that is, the business's customers or clients. And yet, given the central role of the customer in what is a very simple model, many businesses neglect to devote time and attention to understanding who their customers are, why they buy, and—very importantly—why they don't buy. Those small business owners who take the time to dig deep often find keys to unlocking success by focusing on sales and marketing strategies.

Your customers may need to see a change in what you offer for sale, how you offer it, or opportunities to support a stronger customer relationship through other aspects of your business, like product knowledge or after-sales service and follow up. Your customers hold the key to unlocking ways to build better value—no matter what product or service you offer. It comes down to finding better ways to hear what they are telling you, listening carefully to the insights they provide, then responding to the opportunities they identify in a way that distinguishes your business in a competitive marketplace.

How do you keep in touch with your customers? Do you have a process to regularly connect with them and evaluate what they may be telling you? It's the critical first step in building an effective sales and marketing strategy.

UNLOCKING KEY: Understand your customers by creating mechanisms that give you practical information about your customer's likes, dislikes, needs, and preferences.

It takes some time and effort, but here are some ideas we've seen work:

- Be deliberate about being "out front" in your business, talking to your customers about what they like and dislike about your products and services. While you're at it, when your customer has something positive to say, ask if he or she'd be willing to provide a testimonial you can use to support other sales.
- Collect data on your customers' buying preferences. Categorize information based on demographic factors like age and gender, sociographic information like income and seasonality of purchases, and any other information that can help you understand what makes them tick. If you are selling to businesses, what industry are they in? What's the size of the business? What are the issues they are dealing with? Who will be making the key decision to choose you as their supplier?
- Do a survey. It could be as simple as asking a few simple questions when you're face to face with a customer or, at the other end of the scale, employing a consultant who can develop and conduct the survey for you. Either way, make sure your questions get to the key issues that drive a customer's buying decisions. Surveys also provide a great way to track your performance over time. Are your customers more or less satisfied than they were last month or last year? Why?

- Explore mystery shopping, either by asking a friend or relative to shop your competitors, or by hiring a mystery shopper to do it for you. This gives you important insights into what your competitors are doing. Do you see evidence that they understand something about your target customer that you have possibly overlooked?
- Get online. Use the Web to keep up to date with emerging trends. Given our access to information "on demand," there is little excuse for not being informed about the latest and greatest things out there.

Armed with this information, you are now ready to strategically evaluate the potential of various segments that you serve.

UNLOCKING KEY: Identify which of your customer segments has the highest potential to help you achieve your business goals.

Cavendish Figurines Ltd.

Business partners Jeannette Arsenault and Don Maxfield began their business of manufacturing figurines of the well-known characters from *Anne of Green Gables* in P.E.I. in 1989. They soon capitalized on the tourist end of the business, starting with factory tours, then building a gift shop and more, to become a provincial tourist destination.

When a vacationer lamented that the public "Welcome to P.E.I." sign wasn't accessible to take a picture in front of it, Jeannette and Don listened. "We built our own welcome sign on the property to allow our visitors to have a great photo op," said Jeannette. Other attractions include a seven-foot-high statue of Anne of Green Gables, a six-foot tall plush lobster named Lorenzo, as well as the opportunity for men, women, and children to dress up as Anne and have their photos taken. And Cavendish continues to offer free tours of the factory.

Thanks to their strong tourism component, Jeannette and Don quickly recognized that motorcoach businesses were an important niche market for them to target. "We visited the head offices of motorcoach companies and told them why Cavendish should be their first stop." The company continues to do direct mail advertising to thank these companies for their previous business, and to remind them of everything they do to maintain their reputation as a fresh and reliable tourist draw. Visit the company's website at **www.cavendishfigurines.com**.

CUSTOMER SEGMENTS

No business is able to be everything to everyone. Yet there is something tantalizing about pursuing every opportunity that presents itself, seeing everyone as a potential customer, and trying to sell more—no matter what the cost to the business. It's almost counterintuitive to limit your sales and marketing efforts to a specific segment of customers—until you understand the full potential of that segment to generate revenue.

If you have done your customer research, you now have a good understanding of who your customers are, why they buy from you, and their likes and dislikes. Now consider which segments of your customer base offer the highest potential to contribute to your businesses goals. The majority of small business owners tell us the 80/20 rule is true: 80 per cent of their revenue is generated from 20 per cent of their customers. This 20 per cent of customers tend to be the most loyal. Their needs are aligned to the core purpose of the business. They tend to be easier to sell to and easier to service. Eventually, they become your strongest advocates for the business.

So when you consider your customer base, ask yourself the following:

- Is there a segment of your customers who spend more than others? If so, who are they, where do they live, how and when do they buy, and who else do they know that might need what you're selling?
- Do some customers buy more often?
- Do some customers tend to buy products that have a higher markup and contribute more to your bottom line?
- Do some of your customers buy similar products and services from your competitors? This provides you with an opportunity to give them a reason to consolidate their buying through you.
- Do some customers take an inordinate amount of your time for a limited bottom-line return? This could range from being slow to pay invoices to taking an inordinate amount of time to purchase a low-priced widget.

By thinking of your customers in segmented groups, you can identify common attributes to better tailor your sales and marketing strategies, and demonstrate your competitive advantage and how it meets their needs.

Let's consider a new business whose primary service is to

provide information technology solutions to other businesses. They may begin by realizing there are over 2.4 million businesses in Canada and they are all potential customers! However, the technology needs of these businesses vary widely. The solutions our business would have to provide would be drastically different depending on the type of business we serve. What is required for a restaurant is radically different from what is needed for a manufacturer. Pinpointing a specific segment simplifies our efforts significantly. For example, we could choose to serve the technology needs of health-care professionals. This targeting allows our business to better service customers by developing expertise and specialized offers that specifically meet the needs of health-care professionals. We can focus on developing expertise relative to the types of systems doctors and dentists use for billing or for customer records; what equipment is generally used and how it is interconnected; and options to backup important data files and restore them in the event of a disaster. This expertise will increase our ability to provide more cost-effective solutions that will likely lead to more profits.

You can see that when we narrow our focus to local doctor and dentist offices, it becomes much easier to identify appropriate sales and marketing strategies. Now we can consider important aspects of the professionals' buying processes, and tailor our tactics to the opportunity:

- How is the buying decision made? Is it the professional or the office manager who chooses?
- What are their key "pain points," the things that keep them up at night, and can we directly address those issues in our sales pitch?

- Can we partner with equipment providers or other sales people who are also targeting this segment?
- Are there local trade shows that professionals might be attending that we should participate in?
- Should we establish relationships with accountants or other professionals who have a strong client base in the health-care industry?

You can see that when we make the key decision to focus on a specific customer segment, we're able to make our marketing more relevant and increase the likelihood we will attract more business from them.

 UNLOCKING KEY: With the profile of your targeted segment in mind, identify obstacles to increasing sales from your primary prospects, and consider ways to turn those obstacles into advantages to help you close more sales.

THE BUYING PROCESS

Think about the process of buying a product or service from your customer's point of view:

1. Customers have a need.
2. They begin to search out products or services to meet that need.
3. They become aware of the various alternatives.
4. They evaluate each alternative considering:

- their perception of the degree to which each alternative meets the need;
- how easy it is to get the product or service;
- the cost of the alternative; and
- their experience or others' experiences with the provider of the product or service.

5. They make their decision to buy.
6. They use the product or service and form opinions about:
   - how well it meets the need; and
   - their ongoing relationship with the provider of the service relative to after-sales service and advice.
7. They make future decisions about whether to buy again.
8. They tell others about their experience with the product or service, and with you and your business.

By understanding the buying process from the customer's point of view, you can identify any potential obstacles. You can also develop sales and marketing tactics to distinguish your business and position yourself for additional sales—both from this customer and from others who have similar needs. Thinking through each of the elements in this sales process will help you identify potential obstacles in the process and create strategies to overcome those obstacles.

For example, look at the first step in the process: The customer has a need. Now consider issues such as:

- What is the specific need that your customer really has when he buys your product, and does your product or service meet that need? Could a different product mix better meet the customer's need? Should you reposition your marketing material to more clearly meet the expressed customer need?

- Is the customer being driven by needs or wants? Needs tend to be long-term in nature while wants can be more susceptible to changing consumer trends.
- How have these needs changed over time, and have you kept pace with them?
- How are these needs likely to change in the future, and how will you anticipate how those changing needs will affect the products or services you provide?

Stonehame Lodge and Chalets

Jeff and Don Gunn are partners in Stonehame, a unique agritourism company in Scotsburn, Nova Scotia, which started as a farm then diversified. Stonehame currently offers year-round accommodations in ten log chalets as well as seventeen private guest rooms. The site is also a working farm with forage and grain crops, and dairy cows.

A unique market segment opened up in 2000 when guests began asking for the bigger chalets for business meetings. "We built the lodge to attract corporate groups in the off-season," says Jeff. Now corporate groups have become an important target market. In addition to meeting space, Stonehame offers team-building exercises, all in a restful location that gives executives a chance to work in a unique environment.

"It is very important to know your market and what your guests want," Jeff says. "We try to create an experience for them."

While they do a range of marketing to attract new clients, they keep an extensive database to target their existing customers. After all, Jeff says, "it costs five times less to market to existing customers than new ones." Visit the company's website at **www.stonehamechalets.com**.

Once you understand the segment you are targeting, you have a number of options that can help you generate more revenue growth from those customers or potentially look to other groups that may be related. If revenue growth is a key objective for you, consider these different segment strategies and their potential to grow your business:

- Sell to more customers in an existing customer segment. Assuming that you have a clearly defined target customer segment, winning more customers within this group is the most straightforward strategy of all. Basically, it's doing more of what you are doing today and potentially equipping your business with different or additional sales and marketing tactics.
- Sell to a new customer segment. Assuming that you are focused on a distinct customer segment, you can expand your target market to include additional segments. For example, if you have been targeting health-care professionals, you may want to consider other professionals such as accountants, lawyers, or architects.
- Sell new products or services to existing or new customer segments. Are there complementary products or services you can offer? For example, some electronics or computer retailers also sell extended warranties on their products.
- Sell more frequently to existing or new customers. Is there a way to encourage your customers to purchase from you

more often? Coffee cards, where the tenth coffee is free, encourage regular customers to repeat their purchases with the same provider.

• Sell to the same segment but look for new customers in a different geographic location. If you are local, perhaps you can expand to become a larger regional player, or if you are regional, perhaps you can go national; if you're national, think global.

SALES AND MARKETING TACTICS

At this point, you have a clear understanding of what segment you are focusing on. You have assessed obstacles that may impede your prospects' buying decision. You have also considered how you plan to grow your business by leveraging your knowledge and expertise in a particular segment. Now it's time to look at the specific sales and marketing tactics that reinforce your competitive advantage with your targeted segment.

As you consider your options, you will quickly recognize that you can spend a lot of money on marketing. Investing dollars in targeted marketing activities is usually a better investment than broad marketing media such as newspapers or radio.

Focus on Your Sales Force

Your sales force may have a number of people who are selling your product or service. The following questions may identify opporunities to improve their effectiveness:

• Have I established specific sales targets for my sales force, and are there rewards or consequences for meeting or not meeting them? Do we celebrate their achievements in a meaningful way?

- Is my sales force calling on the right sales prospects in the right customer segment? What does their prospect pipeline look like?
- Do we need to provide more marketing support to help them build their prospect pipeline?
- Does my sales force have good customer relationship skills, effectively engaging prospects? Are they able to represent our product or service with the expertise and confidence my customers expect?
- Is my sales force able to close sales? Are they able to identify and address customer concerns? Does my sales force need more training to be more effective?
- Are there ways to make my sales force more productive? Do they operate relatively independently of me, or do I end up spending significant time fixing problems they have created?

Focus on Your Company's Branding

Branding is an essential part of your marketing strategy because, in essence, it succinctly represents your company image. To determine whether you are realizing all the benefits of a successful brand, ask yourself the following questions:

- Have I created a brand image that clearly communicates the value my business delivers? Is it consistent with my competitive advantage? Does it help distinguish me from the competition?

- Does my brand capture attributes my targeted segment recognizes as being significant to them? For example, do I position my business as traditional or innovative, luxury or budget?
- Is my brand consistent, being used repeatedly in all aspects of my business? Consider every point where my business touches a customer. Does my marketing material, business cards, letterhead, website, and the way we interact with each customer leave a positive impression in the customer's mind?

Focus on Advertising

Advertising is how you deliver information about your company, product, or service to potential customers: It can be very expensive. By focusing on some key questions you can ensure that the money you do spend is effective:

- Is my advertising efficient? That is, do I have a strategic process for assessing where I advertise, how often I advertise, and how successful that advertising is?
- Do I measure the results of my advertising by asking my customers or clients where they heard about the business?
- Have I developed clear advertising messages that speak in terms of the benefits my customers will receive as opposed to simply describing who we are?

Focus on Your Online Strategy

These days, most businesses consider whether or not their business would benefit by having an online presence. If you're planning on creating a website or already have one, ask yourself the following:

- What do I want my Web presence to be? Do I want to simply provide information or do I want to actually sell my product or service online?
- Do I keep my website up to date? Does it look professional? As an extension of the business, does it integrate with my broader marketing messages?
- Do I have the time and ability to maintain it myself, or would it be better to hire experts to keep it professional and up to date?

Shin Wa Kan Dojo

Donna Murphy has been a student of martial arts for thirty-two years and a teacher for twenty-two. In 2002, she opened Shin Wa Kan Dojo in St. Catharines, Ontario. The dojo is a martial arts school that teaches traditional, old-style Japanese martial arts. It helps children, youth, and adults achieve their full potential in all aspects of life through the teachings of self-discipline, self-respect, and inner strength. "Our whole approach to teaching is different from most other dojos," says Donna. "I ensure the dojo is a place of encouragement, reinforcing the positive in a nurturing atmosphere. People have enough stress and pressure in their lives—it's not conducive to learning to have that on the mat as well."

She has tried a number of advertising methods over the years and has evaluated their worth to her business. "I spent quite a lot of time and money over the first couple of years in joining business networking groups and attending events," says

Donna. "Although I had a high profile at these events, received a lot of very positive attention, and the events themselves were very well attended, they were unproductive in actually getting people into the dojo as potential students." Nevertheless, she did make a number of excellent contacts with other small business owners in the area.

She initially took out an ad in the Yellow Pages as well as other print directories. "These also had online directories associated with them," says Donna. "Over the next five years or so, I found fewer and fewer callers finding me in the phone book, and more and more finding me on the Internet. So this year I discontinued the hard-copy directories, which are quite expensive, and kept the online directories." She also researched other online directories and signed up for every free one that was available.

Donna has had a website for six years. "I signed up for a Web-hosting service so I could build and manage my own website, which was quite a steep learning curve for me! I was happy with the result. However, there were issues with the template style of website construction, which make it invisible to Google." She is how redeveloping the site.

She also advertised through the popular search engine for a while. "It was arranged by one of my students," says Donna. "That was very productive and I will be looking at resuming that as soon as my new website is ready."

Donna's advice to other small business owners is to monitor your results. "Don't be afraid to pull the plug on unproductive avenues if you've given them enough time but they still aren't showing results," she says. "Don't go on assumptions, and don't hesitate to ask new contacts where they heard of you."

"It's really easy to overspend on advertising, so decide what you can afford, then research the best route to get the most bang for your buck." Visit the company's website at **www.shinwakandojo.com.**

Focus on Building a Database of Customers and Prospects

Your existing customers have helped you build your business. It's important to keep a strong database of their information and buying practices. It's also useful to keep a database of new prospects to market to. Ask yourself:

- Do I know who my customers are? Do I have a comprehensive list that includes details of all of my customers? Do I know what they are buying and how frequently? If they stopped buying from me, would I know?
- Do I use my database to undertake direct marketing initiatives such as direct mail, email, or personal telephone calls?
- Do I ask my most loyal customers for referrals? Have I considered sending them something they could pass along to their friends or colleagues—like a coupon or something free—as a way to invite them to give us a try?
- Have I created a database of prospective customers to whom I can direct targeted marketing campaigns?
- Having built up a prospect database, what tactics am I using to keep it up to date and to keep the new prospect pipeline full?

Focus on Other Marketing Tactics

While focusing on your sales force, branding, advertising, online strategy, and database marketing, there is still a range of other options that may fit your particular type of business. While they may seem a little "out of the box," ask yourself if you can broaden your marketing program by including the following tactics:

- Can I leverage a public relations strategy that positions me and my business as a source of expertise in the community?
- Do I deliberately network to expand my reach to new prospects and get the word out about the products, service, and expertise we offer?
- Have I considered writing articles and offering them to local publications, positioning myself as an expert relative to my industry or service?
- Have I considered trade shows as an alternative way to highlight my product or services?
- Can I partner with other non-competing businesses that are targeting the same segment I am pursuing? Can I offer a complementary product or service to what they offer, and combine my marketing efforts with theirs to reach more prospects?

UNLOCKING KEY: Do an inventory of your sales and marketing strategies and identify those that are delivering results. Explore the possibility of enhancing your marketing program by adopting new tactics that will reach your targeted segment.

Get Growing *for business* **Online Resource:** The Sales and Marketing worksheet takes you through a process of identifying the various segments of your market you could choose to target; evaluating each segment's potential to achieve the goals you have established for your business; identifying the needs and wants of your targeted segment; and identifying appropriate tactics to optimize the results you achieve from the segments you choose to focus on (**www.getgrowingforbusiness. com/unlocking/salesandmarketing**).

3

MANAGING CASH FLOW

Pilates North

In March 2000, twin sisters Rachel and Lisa Schklar took a leap
of faith to start Pilates North. Displaying true entrepreneurial
spirit, they started with just enough money for a month's rent,
five yoga mats, and hardwood flooring (that they installed themselves) for their 700-square-foot studio. They went door to door
signing up people for the studio's Pilates classes—at a time when
Pilates was not the commonly known fitness discipline it is now.

Today, Pilates North runs approximately fifty classes a week.
Their staff of seven trainers—Lisa included—work with a variety of body types, including people with disabilities and professional athletes, out of their 3,000-square-foot studio.

Rachel believes that a vital key to their success is the way
their clients attend classes. Unlike some fitness studios, Pilates
North is entirely registration-based—they don't have drop-in

classes. "This creates a sense of commitment in our clients," says Rachel. "They're more motivated to come to class."

It also plays an essential part in the business's cash-flow strategy. Clients sign up for a series of classes and pay for all of them upfront, which helps the sisters plan out specific aspects of their business based on confirmed registrants. Rachel continually uses her previous experience working with a large clothing store company to do cash-flow planning and sales projections.

"You need to look at your sales and ask the 'what-ifs': What if we don't get the sales? Also, what does it look like this week? This month?" she says. Visit the company's website at **www. pilatesnorth.com**.

Growing businesses consume money. Many have called cash flow the life blood of small business, and it's true. While a great business idea, a passionate entrepreneur, and customers ready to buy are the building blocks of a successful business, cash is the life force that transforms and feeds the potential of the enterprise. It allows it to thrive or, if there is not enough, can make the business anaemic and constrained. In the worst cases, it can ultimately be the factor that ends its existence.

The successful small business owners we met understood the central role of cash flow. They were very deliberate about taking care of their cash. They understood exactly where it was going to come from and where it was going to—and, most importantly, when.

 UNLOCKING KEY: Know exactly when cash will be flowing into or out of your business by doing a cash-flow projection.

THE IMPORTANCE OF CASH-FLOW PLANNING

The good news is that in most cases cash flow is relatively predictable. For example, by looking at those customers who have purchased products or services from your business in the past, you can determine how many have paid you cash immediately, how many have used credit or debit cards, and how many you have granted credit to, in the form of setting up a receivable. You could take it even further and look at those who have had a receivable in the past, and determine who has paid you within thirty, sixty, ninety or more days, or, in some cases, not at all!

When things are predictable, you have the opportunity to plan. Cash-flow plans take advantage of historical realities to project an anticipated future outcome.

You may ask, "How can I rely on the past to predict an uncertain future?" Clearly, future events will have an impact on your projections. However, by making certain assumptions you can explore the impact of those future events on cash-flow outcomes. This is the power of planning. By doing projections that model different assumptions, you can make informed decisions that factor in a wide range of scenarios. You can test different assumptions and see how they play out in a hypothetical planning scenario, as opposed to learning about their consequences in the real world. It's much easier to consider the implications of decisions on a planning spreadsheet than it is to experience the reality of unexpected outcomes when the bank balance is zero.

PROFITS VERSUS CASH

"But I already do a profit and loss statement every month, and it shows that my business is profitable. I don't need to do a cash flow, too."

The reality is that profits don't pay the bills—cash does!

It's important to recognize the difference between profit and cash. Profits are a calculated figure—the difference between revenue and expense as recorded on your business's income statement.

Cash, on the other hand, is a tangible asset of the business. It accumulates in the till, and in your bank account. It is generated from a variety of business activities, including the sale of other assets (like inventory or even old equipment), an increase in liabilities (taking out a loan), as well as from the proceeds of sales. Cash is what will meet the next payroll or pay the fuel bill.

Profits are important, but they will not be available to pay the bills until they turn into cash. Planning cash flow looks at both the sources and uses of cash and the timing of its receipt by the business. Making sure you have enough cash on hand avoids the cash-flow crisis that can occur when you have too much cash going out of your business—and not enough coming in.

ANATOMY OF A CASH-FLOW CRISIS:

Consider this example. Let's say your business had profits of $100,000 last month, and at month-end you have $80,000 in cash in your bank account. You decided you want to reinvest $70,000 of that cash in shiny new inventory that offers the potential to double your investment, generating $140,000 in cash once it's sold. By reinvesting $70,000 you have created the opportunity to increase your profits a further $70,000; however, you have only $10,000 remaining in your bank account once the inventory is purchased. Staff payroll is tomorrow, and it will be $15,000—plus the rent is also due in the amount of $5,000. You now have a cash-flow crisis! There are plenty of profits but not enough cash.

Available cash = $80,000

Buy inventory = $70,000

Pay staff = $15,000

Pay rent = $5,000

Cash shortfall = $10,000

By doing a cash flow projection you can anticipate the consequences of decisions such as purchasing more inventory, extending more generous terms on your receivables, hiring more staff, and so on. Planning lets you make each decision strategically without risking a cash-flow crisis. In our previous example, with a bit of planning you might have reduced your inventory buy to $60,000, avoiding the crisis.

Available cash = $80,000

Buy inventory = $60,000

Pay staff = $15,000

Pay rent = $5,000

Cash shortfall = $0

If you have never done a cash-flow projection in the past, it does take some time and deliberation to do a good one. It's

a matter of taking a careful look at all cash inflows and outflows and the timing of each expense.

CREATING YOUR BUSINESS'S CASH-FLOW PROJECTIONS

There are a number of reasons you will want to do a cash flow
projection:

- To create a day-to-day management resource that allows
  you to monitor your cash position and avoid a cash crisis.
- To project the impact of a planned strategy, such as any of
  the Unlocking Key approaches outlined in this book.
- To create "what-if scenarios" that allow you to plan alternatives to meet cash-flow fluctuations created by market conditions beyond your control, positive or negative.

The first cash-flow projection you prepare is the most difficult. Subsequent forecasts become much easier once you
have a baseline to model from.

If your company has a sources-and-uses-of-cash statement prepared as part of your year-end reporting, you can
see how this report summarizes all the cash in and out of your
business over a full year. The cash-flow projections you will
create will cover shorter periods of time, perhaps monthly or
even weekly. At this level of detail, you will have the information you need to make day-to-day decisions with the benefit
of an accurate and up-to-date cash-flow picture.

You can develop the projections yourself or work with your

accountant. Then, based on your plans and your knowledge of the business, you can figure out how cash flow might change in the next period. This will allow you to arrive at a net cash position for each planning period.

> **Get Growing** *for business* **Online Resources:** A detailed cash-flow planning tool called Scotia Cash Flow *for business*™ allows you to model various cash-flow scenarios and test "what-if" assumptions you may be considering in your business (**www.getgrowingforbusiness. com/unlocking/cashflow**).

From the perspective of considering Unlocking Key strategies, whether you create your cash-flow projections or you work with your accountant to have them completed, this is an important step in the process of preparing your business to grow.

SOURCES AND USES OF CASH

The easiest way to understand how cash flows into and out of your business is by looking at your balance sheet. Every asset or liability listed on your balance sheet is a potential source of cash or a use of cash. For example, when you grant a customer credit in the form of setting up a receivable, the balance sheet category "receivables" will increase.

Think about what this represents. Receivables are not cash until they are paid. So when you set up a receivable for

$100 dollars, you've already captured this as a sale on your income statement, incurred expenses to purchase raw materials, or paid employees who work to manufacture or sell the product. In other words, you've already spent cash before you will receive cash from the sale. So setting up the receivable is a "use of cash" until it is paid, at which time it becomes a "source of cash."

By creating a monthly cash-flow projection, you can quickly identify the sources and uses of your cash in the planning period. Creating monthly projections for the coming year will also enable you to visualize seasonal fluctuations in your net cash position over time. With this information in hand you can begin to identify areas where you may be able to increase sources of cash during periods you need it, and when you will have cash available to spend on specific projects.

Stonehame Lodge and Chalets

We met Jeff Gunn in Chapter 2, and learned how Stonehame has grown its original farming business into an agri-tourism venture. Because farming and tourism are both seasonal businesses, which typically create most of the company's earnings between May and November, it has worked to avoid this seasonality.

"We've worked to bring revenue in at quieter times," says Jeff. The company provides meeting facilities in its lodge and team-building exercises for corporate groups, which is a boon in the off-season.

Stonehame also puts together tourist packages for Christmas and March Break, emailing its database of customers in advance to let them know about the offers. "We are always looking for ways to keep the business growing," Jeff says.

The bottom line on a cash-flow projection is your net-cash position. If it is positive, your sources of cash were greater than your uses of cash during the planning period, and you have a cash surplus. If your uses of cash were greater than your sources of cash, you have a cash shortfall.

You always have a decision to make about your net-cash position. If it is positive and you have a surplus, will you leave the cash in the business? Will you use it to increase assets or reduce liabilities? Will you pay it out to cover expenses? Will you take it out of the business for personal use? If your net cash position is negative and you have a shortfall, will you cover that negative position by reducing assets? Increasing liabilities? Delaying the payment of expenses? Injecting more personal money into the business? These are the immediate decisions you will have to make.

Understand the business factors that create surplus cash or cash shortfalls. To a large extent these factors are predictable and, with realistic cash flow planning, you can respond to either scenario.

UNLOCKING KEY: Make cash-flow planning a central element of the process you use to consider the viability of any strategy you might undertake, and a regular activity as you monitor the results of any initiative you have already undertaken.

PLANNING CASH FLOW TO SUPPORT SALES AND REVENUE GROWTH

Growing a business puts particular strains on cash flow. Increased sales will result in corresponding increases in expenses and various assets, including inventory, receivables, and equipment or premises. If sales increase rapidly, they can quickly outstrip available cash and push the business into a cash crisis. Further, expenses are likely to trend upward from increased salaries or wages as well as all those other day-to-day costs associated with larger operations.

But bigger is better, right? To the extent that increased sales and revenue have the potential to increase profits, most people would conclude that growing revenue is the way to go. However, ensure you are being guided by your key goals. You may, in fact, decide you want to "right size" your business. You may choose to keep sales and revenue at their current levels, and focus on increasing profits. It may make more sense to implement strategies to increase gross profit margins (your markup on a given sale) or reduce expenses. You may choose not to grow because you recognize the increased demands on your personal time or financial resources, as the size of your business inevitably consumes more of each. Choosing to grow sales and revenue is a strategic decision—not a forgone conclusion.

That said, let's assume you've decided you want to pursue the option of increased sales or revenue. As you consider various sales and marketing strategies that will deliver increased revenue, make a point of identifying those areas of your business you will have to change to accommodate the growth. Think through the additional costs that will be associated with the changes then capture those anticipated costs in a revised cash-flow forecast that incorporates changes in revenue, increases in balance sheet items, and increased expenses. You must consider all three to have an accurate picture of what your net cash position will be.

UNLOCKING KEY: Anticipate the impact of planned sales and revenue growth by preparing a cash flow projection that incorporates not only the increased cash contribution of higher levels of revenue but also the increased cash required to fund balance-sheet items and increased expenses.

Whether you've adopted a sales and revenue growth strategy or have decided to take a "right size" approach, two line items on your balance sheet have particular significance in any cash-flow planning. They have a reputation for derailing some of the best made business plans. Those assets are receivables and inventory.

Small business owners we met who understood the central role of receivables and inventory in the sales cycle and their effect on cash flow tended to be able to anticipate and avoid cash-flow crises.

THE SALES CYCLE

In the process of selling a product or delivering a service there is a sequence to the sales process that requires an investment of cash:

1. Acquiring a product or developing a service available to purchase.

2. Offering the product or service for sale and making that sale.
3. Delivering the product or service.
4. Receiving cash payment for the product or service.

This process takes time to complete, and every phase of the process requires the investment of cash and resources before cash is ultimately received in payment. It is the timing of these outlays of cash—prior to receipt of cash from the buyer—that requires the commitment of adequate cash to fund the cycle. By adopting strategies that address the various phases of the process, a business owner can significantly affect the amount of cash that must be invested in the sales cycle in order to achieve a given level of sales or revenue.

MANAGING INVENTORY

In the first phase of the sales cycle, the business acquires merchandise or raw material that it will eventually offer for sale. Whether the business delivers professional services, manufactures a product, or retails the product to end consumers, there is usually some aspect of the business that requires inventory to support the sales process. As businesses pursue strategies to increase sales, there is a natural need to rely on higher levels of inventory. Because inventory requires the investment of cash to acquire it, and because there is a period of time between the payment of cash to acquire the inventory and the sale that ultimately returns the cash to the business, significant cash-flow management issues can be created.

The successful small business owners we met realized that even small changes to their inventory practices had a material impact on their cash flow. For example, consider a business with $400,000 in sales last year. This business paid $200,000 for the goods that were sold and maintained three months of inventory. If this business could reduce inventory levels to hold only two months' worth, it would accelerate cash flow by $16,667. This is money the business can use to reduce credit or to invest. Lets look at the math:

Cost of inventory used over twelve months = $200,000
Average inventory used each month ($200,000 ÷ 12) = $16,667

If we choose to keep three months of inventory on hand, we will need to commit $50,001 to maintaining this inventory level. If we reduce inventory on hand to two months supply we will commit only $33,334, saving $16,667 in cash flow.

The businesses with the greatest success in managing their inventory levels manage both the size and makeup of inventory they have on hand as well as the length of time between acquisition of the inventory and its sale. They have created strategies to ensure they have the right inventory at the right time, while keeping it moving off the shelves quickly and in good condition.

UNLOCKING KEY: Consider all elements in the process of acquiring, maintaining, and distributing inventory in order to most efficiently utilize the cash you have invested.

The business owners we talked to used a variety of approaches to optimize their investment in inventory. The importance of effective inventory management was highlighted by the reality that, for some retailers, inventory accounted for as much as 80 per cent of their total current assets, requiring corresponding investments of cash flow. For many, inventory also depreciates over time—just ask computer or electronics distributors or seasonal fashion apparel companies. Here are some of the key strategies they suggest to get the most out of their inventory investment.

Watch the Turns

Your inventory turns measure the number of times that inventory cycles over each year. It's calculated by dividing the total cost of goods sold in a year by the average inventory level.

- Calculate your inventory turns by product or product line to identify fast and slow movers.
- Use inventory tracking systems, such as point-of-sale (POS) software programs, that give you detailed, up-to-date information.
- Research best-in-class inventory-turn benchmarks for similar businesses, and compare your results.

Open-to Buy-Plans

Open-to-buy (OTB) plans are an important part of good inventory control. OTB can be calculated in units or dollars.

- Most applicable for retail stores, first establish a base inventory level at which you are fully stocked.

- Identify your total annual sales based on average-sales benchmarks, or your previous year's actual sales plus anticipated growth and inflation.
- Divide total annual sales by months, and build in seasonal fluctuations by weighting your projections to match historical trends.
- Purchase inventory as frequently as possible (monthly is best, but no less frequently than quarterly in most cases), allowing appropriate time for delivery and stocking.
- Project cash-flow needs based on your open-to-buy plan, and add an appropriate cushion for unplanned buying needs (say 10 per cent).

Just-in-Time Practices

This inventory strategy helps to reduce the length of time you hold your inventory—and the costs associated with carrying it.

- Buy and ship inventory as close to the sale date as possible.
- Anticipate seasonal variations by tracking historical purchasing patterns.
- Adopt purchasing policies that buy only enough inventory to cover sales to the anticipated first markdown date plus a modest projected ending inventory (in case sales are better than anticipated), yet that can be quickly disposed of at a reasonable markdown without creating dead inventory.
- Maintain strong relationships with suppliers to get preferred and quick access to goods that are selling faster than you anticipated.

Watch Your Sales Per Square Foot

Sales per square foot is calculated by dividing your total net sales by the number of square feet of selling space.

- Research appropriate sales-per-square-foot data for similar businesses and create a target benchmark for sales per square foot.
- Use sales projections to establish appropriate inventory levels (sales by targeted turns).
- When sales per square foot do not achieve targeted goals, revisit your merchandising strategies and product mix.

Sales Weighting

You can establish appropriate sales weighting by simply determining which products make you the most money.

- Identify your first, second, and third bestselling items based on bottom-line contribution. Remember, the highest-priced items may not necessarily generate the highest profits.
- Assign larger, more prominent in-store positions to higher-ranked products.
- Focus any in-store advertising or promotions to your highest-ranked products.
- Plan your inventory around the higher exposure you plan for higher-ranked products.

Managing Dead Inventory

Inventory that is not selling is a dead weight in your business, adding costs and holding cash that could better be spent else-where.

- Let your targeted turns guide you as you manage mark-downs to eliminate dead inventory. If your target is six turns, a two-month shelf life is your objective. Consider starting markdowns at six weeks, and adopt policies that set out when and how much subsequent reductions should be.
- Remember dead inventory not only ties up cash flow in dusty, non-contributing assets, but also eliminates the opportunity to reinvest those dollars in your highest-performing inventory.

Financing Your Inventory

Depending on the industry you are in, there may be a variety of alternatives to finance your inventory, each with different cash-flow implications.

- Suppliers often offer credit terms. Consider the cost of these alternatives against traditional bank financing by annualizing the benefit of any foregone discounts for cash purchases. Remember, you will be able to negotiate better terms when you have a good credit history and solid busi-ness results.
- Is product available on consignment? Again, what terms are offered while you wait for a sale to materialize, and what discounts would be available if you purchased the inventory outright?
- Supplier-managed inventory plans are available in some

industries, whereby inventory is purchased at a fixed price but delivered and invoiced at a future date as needed by your business.

Get Growing *for business* Online Resource: The Inventory Management worksheet helps to identify inventory strategies that increase the likelihood your business will have the right inventory to meet your customers' needs, while minimizing the cash-flow impact. When used in combination with the "what-if" capabilities of the Scotia Cash Flow *for business* tool, you can test the implications of various inventory strategy alternatives (**www.getgrowingforbusiness.com/unlocking/cashflow**).

Ingrained Style Furniture Company

Mike and Alisen Dopf began Ingrained Style (originally known as The Pine Shop) in Calgary, Alberta, in 1996. They set themselves apart from competitors that offer mass-produced furniture imported from halfway around the world by creating custom pieces that they produce themselves using quality craftsmanship.

The company ran into a challenge when the Alberta economy began to boom. The cost of labour doubled, even tripled, and good people became hard to find. For nearly two years they were unable to hire. "We needed a more efficient system to work with the employees we had," says Alisen.

The Dopfs saw that they were maintaining a large inventory of furniture and raw materials. They decided to sell off their inventory and began to streamline their process. Selling the inventory increased their cash flow immensely, and had the added benefit of reducing the amount of leased space that was necessary.

Their sales cycle has been simplified. First, they work with the customer to create the custom design. When the customer places the order, Ingrained takes a 50 per cent deposit and orders the raw materials. By streamlining the production process, if the Dopfs order the raw materials on a Monday, the product is typically ready to be shipped out on Friday of the same week—when they receive the rest of the payment. This keeps their receivables low and allows for greater cash flow. Visit the company's website at **www.ingrainedstyle.com**.

MANAGING RECEIVABLES TO OPTIMIZE CASH FLOW

In many cases, the decision to pursue growth in your business may bring you to the point of deciding whether or not to grant credit terms to customers. It can be an effective way to accommodate your customer's desire to buy more, but it has some inherent risks. If you choose to grant credit, you will need to understand how to manage the resulting receivables in such a way as to reduce the possibility of loss due to non-payment. Recognize the implications of not having access to the cash from these sales until the receivable is ultimately paid. In other words, you will have to focus on creating an appropriate receivables strategy.

This was a common source of tension for many of the businesses owners we met, particularly in industries in which setting up customer accounts to facilitate credit sales was a common practice. It becomes particularly critical for growing enterprises, as both the number of receivables that need to be managed and the total dollars increased. Understanding how receivables will affect cash flow is an important part of growing your business. Receivables have the potential to effectively support growth when well managed or, conversely, create a minefield of risks.

When customers make the decision to buy your product or service they will be weighing a number of factors specific to what you offer for sale (for example, quality, ability to deliver anticipated benefit, and price) as well as service-related issues (for example, knowledgeable and friendly staff, and after-sales service). They will also be considering how they will pay you—and when. As you refine how your business will unlock its growth potential, you need to carefully consider how you want to deal with customer payments, and the pros and cons of setting up customer accounts that allow you to grant credit terms. So the first decision is: Does my business grant credit?

In a competitive marketplace, some businesses experience a great deal of pressure to "pay later"; one way for your customers to do that is to ask you to set up a receivable. Simply put, they want you to give them the product right away, and give you the cash later.

The decision to establish a receivable is a strategic one. You must weigh:

- the cash-flow impact of delivering the product now and receiving the cash later;
- the expense of carrying those receivables, whether in the form of interest on loans to fund the receivable (remember it's just like buying any other balance sheet asset—you

must pay for it!) or the loss of use of cash flow that is tied
up in those receivables;

- the consequence of not granting the receivable in terms of
lost sales opportunities, particularly if your competitors
offer a "pay later" solution;
- the potential risk that your customer does not ultimately
pay you either because they choose not to, or are unable to
do so; and
- other alternatives that avoid setting up the receivable may
be available, such as accepting credit cards (which transfer
the collection risk to the credit-card company for a fee).

If you've made the decision to grant credit to your customers in the form of a receivable, there are a variety of strategies you can use to help ensure those receivables get turned
into cash in a predictable and timely way. They include:

- creating an application form that gathers contact information, and provides authorization to obtain a credit report;
- clearly communicating the terms of payment and any
consequences for not meeting those terms;
- using an accounting system that allows you to track outstanding receivables and flags any overdue accounts for
immediate follow up;
- regularly scheduling collection activities, and assigning
both specific times and responsibilities for the task;
- not granting any further credit when a customer fails to
meet repayment terms; and
- considering using third parties to handle difficult collection situations.

Get Growing *for business* Online Resource: A template of a credit application as a cash-flow management resource that can be adapted for use in your business (www.getgrowingforbusiness.com/unlocking/cashflow).

There is an inherent risk whenever you agree to accept payment after delivery of the product or service. Essentially, you are exposing your company to the possibility your customers will not be able to pay. You are now indirectly exposed to any risks in their business.

Further, you are trying to determine which customers will pay and which ones will not on the basis of limited information. It is difficult to get it right all the time and it is the rare small business that does not end up with uncollectable accounts. When these are written off they become a direct cost, reducing your net profit dollar for dollar. The problems your customers may be having that lead to these write-offs can be specific to that particular customer, which is bad enough, but during economic downturns a whole sector may be affected, which may potentially affect all your receivables at a time when your business could be struggling with other aspects of a challenging market.

Understand that you have the alternative of not granting credit. Even in businesses that operate in industries that traditionally set up receivables, you can make the decision to accept only cash, debit, or credit-card payments. If you choose not to offer credit terms, you will need to assess the advantages (reduced costs for write offs, receivable administration, and collections) against the disadvantages (the potential loss of customers that demand credit, and any fees that will result from increased use of debit- and credit-card payments). How do you make this strategic decision? As with any other similar decision, research the topic, understand the implications for your business from a sales-and-operations point of view, and assess the cash-flow implications by testing the alternatives using cash-flow projections.

If you do decide to grant credit, some simple strategies that can have a material impact in reducing the cash-flow impact of your accounts receivable.

- Consider upfront partial payments, such as a 50 per cent down payment.
- Invoice as soon as you deliver the product or service. Consider hand-delivering the invoice or emailing it to expedite the process.
- Consider the terms of payment (for example, payment is due in ten or fifteen days from receipt of invoice). Think about small discounts, such as 1 per cent, if payment is received in an accelerated manner.
- If the customer pays by cheque, deposit it immediately.

These straightforward tactics may have a significant impact on cash flow. If your business has $400,000 in annual sales, and you can accelerate payment of those receivables—reducing the average day's sales outstanding from thirty-five to thirty days—you will have increased available cash by approximately $5,500. Here's the math:

Total annual sales = $400,000

Average daily sales ($400,000 ÷ 365) = $1,095

At thirty-five-days sales, your receivables will total $38,325 ($1095 × 35) and will reduce to $32,850 ($1095 × 30) at thirty-days sales, generating $5,475 in additional cash flow.

UNLOCKING KEY: Consider both the positive and negative impact of granting receivables, and create a cash-flow projection that models both alternatives. If you do decide to offer credit, establish specific policies for granting, tracking, and collecting your accounts.

Get Growing *for business* **Online Resource:** The Receivables worksheet guides your consideration of the risk and cash-flow implications of granting credit as a strategy to increase sales, and provides a framework to consider key points prior to modelling "what-if" scenarios using the Scotia Cash Flow *for business* tool (**www.getgrowingforbusiness.com/unlocking/cashflow**).

Base Technology Ltd.

Davin Peterson's company, Base Technology Ltd., delivers fully supported high-speed wireless networks. The company is on the move: In 2008, it served more than 10,000 individual customers.

Base Technology is unique in that it owns and operates its wireless network. The company builds its own equipment, installs and maintains the network, and hasdeveloped Web-based software for network management and customer billing.

"Having this kind of end-to-end control over our operations allows us to offer competitive pricing and to act quickly to take advantage of opportunities in a market that didn't exist a few years ago," says Davin.

Base takes full advantage of the Internet to ensure that the company is paid—and paid quickly. "We have developed a hosted website and network management system for handling real-time payments over our wireless network. This has allowed us to immediately collect revenue from all of our subscribers and cover operating costs for the other services we provide," he says. "Customers pay for our service directly through our website with their credit cards. We also invoice business customers on a monthly and quarterly basis." Visit the company's website at **www.basetechnology.net**.

MANAGING EXPENSES

As a business grows, its total expenses increase, requiring more cash as a result. Cost management will be fully explored in Chapter 4; however, it is necessary to briefly mention it here to highlight its implication on cash flow.

As a business becomes more complex, it creates both a challenge and an opportunity from a cost-management point of view.

- The challenge: to effectively manage more expenses across increasingly complex systems.
- The opportunity: to benefit from the efficiencies made possible by an increased scale of enterprise.

Often, the process of effectively managing those expenses will not only require more efficient management systems that allow better expense control, but also provide better information to support decision making.

From a cash-management perspective, creating reliable expense management systems allows the business to anticipate the cash-flow implications of any strategic alternative that may be implemented.

Consider a manufacturer that launched a new computer-controlled lathe to produce a new component for the airline industry. During the early days of bringing the equipment on-line, the cost of training, higher defect rates in the production process, and increased travel and accommodation expenses to stay close to the customer and understand their needs as they tested the new component all required an investment of cash flow—with the ultimate goal of creating a sustainable, profitable product that would contribute to the bottom line for years to come. Recognizing how much cash needed to be invested upfront was part of the cash-flow management process. Creating expense-management strategies that increased the contribution margin over time allowed the company to quantify the long-term profit potential as the process became standardized.

UNLOCKING KEY: Create internal processes that identify required expenses and create appropriate budgets that provide for the estimated costs. Anticipate the cash flow required to support those costs, factoring in both total dollars and timing of cash inflows and outflows.

PLANNING FOR THE UNPLANNED

While on our cross-Canada tour, we spoke with one business owner about how cash flow is the life blood of a healthy business. He made a great point: He reminded us that a blood analysis can also provide an early indication of hidden diseases! Using cash-flow clues can sometimes give you a head start on dealing with the unexpected.

So how do you make provisions for those times when cash flow becomes impaired by any number of inevitable business ailments? What do you do when the unexpected happens?

Here are some of the best ideas we heard:

- Quickly identify any deviations from your cash-flow plan, and respond by identifying the sources of variation right away with decisive actions that address the underlying cause.
- Always be conservative in estimating your cash flow. When planning, delay the anticipated *receipt* of a source of cash by a day or two, and accelerate the anticipated date of a given *use* of cash.
- Always have a plan B, whether it be unused funds in an operating line of credit, a liquid investment in the business, or a personal backup plan. Whatever the source of funds, it should be available on short notice. What's considered a reasonable buffer? It will be different for each business depending on the variability of cash flow and the market demand that fuels the enterprise. For some it may be two weeks' worth of cash, for others it could be as much as six months' worth.

- At a very minimum, make sure you have enough cash on hand or accessible, to pay your essential expenses and outlays, such as payroll, for a period of time.

As with any other aspect of your business, cash flow can be effectively managed. Take a proactive approach to planning and monitoring your cash flow. Use cash-flow models to anticipate issues and create solutions that will ensure your growth potential is not derailed by a cash-flow crisis.

4

CONTROLLING COSTS

Windward Flutes

Yola and Forbes Christie have attracted worldwide attention to the beautiful handcrafted instruments they create at Windward Flutes. Yola was trained in silversmithing and design at the Rhode Island School of Design and through apprenticeships abroad. Forbes is recognized internationally as an accomplished metal flute-maker by concert flautists. The duo built their flute-making facility from 2004–2005.

They recognized the importance of improving their production capacity to reduce costs. "Our market advantage—product quality—depends on precision measurements," says Yola. "The greatest time thief in our manufacturing process is the frequency of stops on the lathe in order to measure the work in progress using handheld calipers." She approximates that over the course of one hundred minutes, the actual manufacturing time is only twenty minutes. The remaining eighty minutes are spent stopping and starting the lathe, measuring the cuts they've made, and doing tool changes and setup.

They sought financing to purchase a precision lathe with a digital readout screen. This way, "the lathe continues to turn right up to the point when the piece reaches the desired measurement," says Yola. "No stopping, no bending, no calculating. This would save ten to fifteen hours per flute." They also needed to add a mill with a motorized bed to increase speed and comfort in the manufacturing process, as well as improve focus by the operator.

They received their new equipment in late 2008 and worked out some electronic and motor problems early in 2009 before self-training began. "After about a month to evaluate the performance of the new tools and the benefits provided by the upgrade, the results are beyond our expectations," says Yola. "We are making more instruments of higher quality, with less physical wear and tear on the artisans, in the same amount of time. Plus, the old lathe is available for use by a second person to perform roughing jobs on flute blanks without cutting into time needed for precision work on the new lathe."

Although adding this equipment will cost them money in the short term, it is improving efficiency, creating less cost per flute in the long term. Visit the company's website at **www. windwardflutes.com.**

You have to spend money to make money, but most successful businesses are very strategic about their spending. They focus on spending less to make a given dollar in profits; it's all about minimizing the costs and maximizing the benefits.

There are two parts to any discussion about managing

costs; the ever-present partner of cost reduction is benefit optimization. Think of it this way: your business must deliver top-quality products, and outstanding service and expertise, and build long-term loyalty with your customer base. In a competitive market, these elements are non-negotiable in order to unlock the potential in your business.

The question then becomes: how do I deliver these non-negotiable elements in an effective way—for the lowest cost?

PLANNING TO MANAGE COSTS

We return to planning, that overarching principle that is a key to success. With your business goals clearly established and your strategies and tactics defined, you will need to make the investment in the resources necessary to implement them. These resources will have a cost, which will vary based on a number of factors—most of which you control. Ultimately, the total sum of those costs will be deducted from the proceeds of the price your customers are willing to pay for your product or service. The difference will be your profit—or your loss if the value is negative.

Planning is actually a system that can be easily represented as a repeatable process:

1. Identify goals.
2. Create strategies.
3. Define tactics.
4. Deploy resources.
5. Sell the product or service.
6. Realize a profit.

Cost planning looks at each element of this system and asks the question: how can I reduce the cost of one aspect of the process or make the whole system more efficient?

In this model, the ultimate reflection of success is the degree to which you can increase profits. Be sure to understand that when you modify one part of a process, you affect another element downstream. So, for example, if you change a tactic, it will require a different set of resources, which have a different cost. It will likely result in a different level of sales and deliver a different level of profit. Look at each element in the process and understand how it affects interrelated aspects of the system.

When you're creating a plan to manage costs, it's particularly important to understand the way that all these steps in the process interact. As an example, investing additional resources in after-sales service will have a cost. However, it will likely also have an impact on your revenue, as you may be justified in charging more for the product or service, or you may receive additional sales from increasingly loyal customers or from new customers they refer.

Planning lets you take a considered approach to the various elements of the business model. By doing so you can:

- test the implications of various strategies and tactics on profits and cash flow;
- isolate the costs of resources that will be required to carry out the tactics you are considering;
- consider various alternatives from different perspectives, including cost, quality, reliability, and service; and
- consider the impact of timing on the sales or production sequence.

Your various alternatives will translate into financial projections. These will explore the impact of any given alternative on both your profit (using a pro forma profit and loss statement), and on your cash flow (using a cash-flow projection). Be sure to factor in all interrelated aspects, including not only the direct costs of resources, but also the secondary effects of, for example, accommodating higher level of sales with increased staffing and training.

Your business plan becomes the baseline for assessing the financial projections of your alternative strategies and tactics. For example, consider increasing your sales force by one person. There is the obvious impact of the salesperson's salary and/or commission. However, there are also additional costs such as supplying them with equipment or technology, their office premises, their day-to-day expenses such as mileage, their use of stationary and telephones, and so on. These costs can be factored into your business plan. There are also intangible costs such as your time required to manage an additional sales resource. These costs need to be contrasted against estimates of the incremental revenue the salesperson will generate. Cash flow is also an important factor as most of these costs will be realized before the revenue is collected. The decision to hire an additional salesperson can be compared against other alternatives such as investing in technology to make your existing sales staff more productive or partnering with a non-competing company for referrals (and maybe even paying them a commission for the referral).

As we stressed in Chapter 1, it's important to avoid the temptation to jump to conclusions in the planning process and prematurely commit to one alternative. You will need to invest some time in order to identify and research various alternatives, as well as forecast the related costs, and the impact on your ability to generate sales and ultimately improve profits. When done thoroughly, effective planning reduces the chances of pursuing a costly alternative that may have unintended consequences.

EXPENSE MANAGEMENT SYSTEMS

Good information is a cost manager's best friend because it increases the likelihood of making good decisions. It relies on the creation and maintenance of systems to identify and track various resources invested in a given business process.

It costs you money to produce your product or service. To understand exactly where those costs come from, you need to construct a cost-management system. It can be as simple as a tally sheet or as complex as sophisticated, automated information-management systems.

Begin by identifying what revenue or expense items need to be measured. Then implement systems that will track them effectively. Always be sure to clearly establish policies and processes that make it clear who does the tracking, when they do it, and how.

Consider the example of an electrician with multiple jobs in different locations. She is looking for ways to increase her profits and recognizes she doesn't have a good handle on her costs. Her first step is to set up a system to track items such as the:

- hours she spends at each job;
- time she spends travelling between jobs;

- number of kilometres she travels in a day;
- quantity of supplies used on a job, and any wasted materials; and
- incremental costs, like telephone, meals, etc.

With this type of accurate information in hand, she can make decisions about the effectiveness of running multiple projects, the potential to reduce costs by changing how she schedules time at, and between, each location, and costing information that will help her price out future contracts more effectively.

Once you have collected data over a period of time, you will have created a baseline of your specific costs. This will allow you to create more accurate projections to support your planning. Depending on the level of detail you're looking for, you may want to convert those projected costs into daily, weekly, quarterly, and annual budgets.

With a good understanding of historic and projected costs, you can identify the cost categories that stray from your budgets. This will allow you to quickly make any necessary adjustments to your business processes. Where adjustments are not possible, you will need to make changes to the financial projections, capturing the new cost realities.

You may also want to benchmark your costs against others in your industry. Trade publications or associations may be able to provide reference resources that report industry standards. Every business is different, however, so it's important to use benchmarks carefully. For example, if your competitive advantage is the quality of your product or service, you should expect your costs to be higher than industry averages.

With good information available, you are better equipped

to make informed decisions about processes in your business. Combine the information from cost-management information systems with data from other systems, such as customer-traffic counts or satisfaction surveys. With a complete picture of the various aspects of your business, including costs, you will be better equipped to make effective decisions. Good decisions increase the likelihood that you will optimize the benefits of your investments.

FIXED AND VARIABLE EXPENSES

Not all costs are created equal. You will have greater control over some expenses than others. This variability is due in part to the type of business you are in and the choices you have made about how you operate your business.

From a cost-management point of view, expenses are either fixed or variable. Fixed expenses are exactly that, fixed. They will not change with different levels of sales. They usually arise from the acquisition of long-term assets or from contractual obligations with a fixed cost. They have the advantage of being predictable, and as sales rise these costs will not increase in lockstep with higher revenue levels. For example, when you buy a piece of equipment and finance it at fixed interest rates over a long term, you will pay the same monthly cost no matter what the level of sales. There may come a point at which you will need to consider acquiring more equipment if your sales grow sufficiently, but the cost of the first piece of equipment will be fixed.

Variable expenses are directly related to sales. As sales go up, so do expenses. Inventory costs are a good example of variable expenses tied to sales.

Fixed Expenses	**Variable Expenses**
Rent	Inventory
Equipment Lease	Hourly Wages
Vehicle Lease	Office Supplies
Insurance	Telephone
Management Salary	Utilities
Internet Access	Gas
	Shipping Costs

In planning, both fixed and variable expenses are controllable. The difference is *when* you control them. With a fixed expense your control is at the point when you commit to the purchase or contract. Long-term asset acquisitions—like equipment—with their associated fixed expenses can offer an important element of predictability. In many cases, they can reduce your costs over the long term. However, they also limit your ability to change strategies once you've made the initial commitment. You are stuck with your choice for the long haul, for better or worse. Ultimately, the choice may work to your advantage if your plans unfold as you expect, or it may work against you if things change.

With variable expenses, you have more options when it comes to adapting to changing circumstances. However, you will need to give up some of the cost benefits of potentially lower-cost long-term arrangements, and their inherent predictability.

As you consider various strategies and tactics, and make choices about how to execute them, be sure to recognize and consider the implications of both fixed and variable expenses to your overall plan. Also consider your ability to adapt to changing circumstances while keeping costs in check.

MANAGING COSTS WITH THE FUTURE IN MIND

Whether it's making existing processes more efficient or managing new tactics that will contribute to long-term profitability, effective cost-management programs make sure the available resources of a business are put to the best use. The best cost-management systems do not restrict growth, they facilitate it.

It's about making choices. The cost of training, research and development, and activities that support positive customer relationships such as community involvement all have long-term benefits for your business.

Ideally, there will be sufficient cash to invest in strategies with both short- and long-term payoffs. However, it is rare to find businesses that have sufficient cash flow to do it all, particularly during difficult economic times.

How do you make the difficult choices when there are limited resources to manage? It's critical to align your investments with your business plan, investing in those capabilities that support your competitive advantage. If your advantage is the level of expertise you provide to customers, training to reinforce this benefit may be a key investment opportunity. If your advantage is price, it may be wise to invest in technology or equipment to reduce your cost per unit.

When expense management decisions are guided by your business goals and aligned to protect and enhance competitive advantages, you will find it easier to make choices that minimize cost structures while investing in the tactics to achieve your key objectives. At the same time, you'll be able to cancel or defer costs for lower-priority initiatives.

On our cross-Canada tour, the successful owners we talked to had a clear understanding of where they were spending their money and how it was contributing to their business. We met a number of manufacturers that used an incredible level of sophistication to measure their per-unit costs. They had defined processes to capture this information and act on it. These small business owners realized it was a journey, not a one-time event. They knew that changes to their process might impact the quality of their products. So they prioritized their changes and isolated each one to study its impact. When they were comfortable, they tested another change, and so on. As they went through the process, they gradually reduced costs, thereby increasing their profit margin.

Successful service businesses also tracked their costs. We met several restaurant owners who were very strategic about their investment in staff, premises, ingredients, and so on. They were aware of the impact each expense had on their customers' experience and balanced it against their gross margin.

KEEPING COSTS UNDER CONTROL

We've discussed how effective cost management requires a combination of planning, information gathering, analysis, and decision making. The lowest-cost alternative may not always be the best one. It's more about making careful, well-informed choices than about spending fewer dollars. Avoid the mistake of letting available cash make decisions for you.

Cost management is about planning to make the best use of the cash available, while factoring in the short- and long-term goals of your business.

Here are some examples of specific approaches to cost control you might want to consider.

Use a Request-for-Quote Process

If you were going to buy a new pair of shoes, you wouldn't just buy the first pair you saw without considering price or size. Likewise, it's important to create a process whenever you need to purchase a new product or service for your business, to ensure you're getting it at a fair cost and that any other requirements are a good fit for your company.

- Create a request for a quote that outlines your requirements for a specific item or service your business needs to purchase.
- Circulate the request by mail, fax, or email, and request quotes from a number of potential suppliers.
- Narrow the field to two or three alternatives. Don't base your decision on price alone. Do your research on the companies' quality, after-sales service, and reputation before finalizing the deal.

Partner with Non-Competing Businesses

It's always a win-win situation when companies can work together to save money or pool resources. You can increase your buying power by partnering with non-competing businesses in a variety of ways:

- Share the cost savings of buying products in higher quantities with other businesses in the vicinity.
- Reduce advertising costs by sharing advertising space, mailing costs, or creative with another business that has a related but non-competing product. For example, a hotel might package advertising with a local restaurant and a tourism attraction.
- Cross-sell with other businesses. For example, a paint retailer can promote a nearby company's decor products by displaying them in the store, and the decor store can show the paint colours that go well with the home accents it sells.

Bartering for Services

There is an increasingly active market in which businesses are trading services to reduce the cost of acquisition. Explore these groups in your local community or online. Remember that even though money is not changing hands, taxes are still payable.

Be on the Lookout for Discounts

There are a variety of ways that businesses can save money on the products and services they buy:

- Consider joining buying groups.
- Contact your local or national business associations as well as any that relate to the products or services you sell. Many provide access to specific benefit programs.
- Search the Web. Be deliberate about finding less well known alternatives that can lower your costs.

Consider Outsourcing

When unusual demands arise due to seasonal volumes or short-term initiatives, outsourcing may be your best option. This way you are using temporary resources to meet demand, rather than making the commitment to purchase equipment or hire additional staff.

Compare Your Costs

Don't assume that your costs must be what they are. Use outside information to compare your costs to others':

- Leverage your advisers to identify opportunities to reduce your costs. For example, if your accountant specializes in your industry, ask how your costs compare against his or her other clients'. Often, coaches or mentors with experience in your industry can help you identify opportunities to reduce your costs.
- Request benchmarks from industry associations and compare them against your costs.

Managing Costs: A Word for Start-Ups

Forecasting future costs (and for that matter revenue) can be very difficult when you are constructing your business plan. It is very easy to underestimate the costs your business will incur. It's like moving into a brand-new house. You incur costs you didn't foresee. Some of them, such as a furnace upgrade or a new appliance, only became apparent after you've lived there for a while. Similarly, after you start your business, there will be additional and unanticipated costs that can consume your available cash. It's important to be conservative in all your forecasted costs. In addition, ensuring you have access to cash, or a strategy to handle the unexpected and inevitable surprises, will help. Also, your adviser team can help identify some of the most common costs to aid you in fine-tuning your business plan.

Chocolate Barr's Candies Inc.

Derek Barr opened the doors to Chocolate Barr's Candies in 2003, just days after his wedding to wife Jacqueline. The sweet shop offers handmade chocolates and other confections to the tourists who visit the picturesque downtown area of Stratford, Ontario. "We're in a great location with great foot traffic," says Derek. Despite the seasonality of the tourism trade, the company maintains steady business all year round by attracting local residents, with a boom at Christmas when it does almost 50 per cent of its sales.

In addition to looking at traditional ways of cutting costs in the business, like new processes or machines to help speed up production, Derek stresses the importance of hard work. "Don't get into a business believing you don't have to work," he says. Whether it's doing your own books, soldering your own pipes, or laying your own flooring, "it's important to do as much as possible yourself to save money."

"To save on costs, I try to do as much of the maintenance as I can. Our enrober—the machine that does the coating—needs to be taken completely apart at least once a year to check the seal and bearings." Derek does this task himself, as it can get very pricey to have a technician come in, especially since some of the machines come from Europe. "The only time that I wasn't able to correct a problem it cost me €3,000—yes euros—not dollars," he says. Visit the company's website at **www.chocolatebarrs.com**.

Keep in mind that cost management is an ongoing process that becomes a part of all aspects of your business planning and day-to-day management. New expenses crop up all the time. Existing processes become inefficient. Be sure to set up periodic reviews to go over your costs and see where you can trim or where you need to invest more to support future growth. With good cost-management practices in place, you'll ensure that you take full advantage of the profit potential in your business.

5

MANAGING YOUR FINANCES

KIVA Design Build

Husband and wife team Doug Glancy and Kiera Newman run
KIVA Design Build Inc. from Niagara Falls, Ontario, designing
and creating outdoor projects for clients from Vancouver to
Montreal to New York. The company is a full-service landscape
design firm—from concept right through to installation.

The couple embrace their individual strengths, bringing a
wide spectrum of abilities to the business. Kiera uses her media
relations and marketing skills to promote the venture. Doug is
the lead landscape designer. He is certified through the CLD
(Certified Landscape Designer) program, and has taught at
both Niagara College and the prestigious Niagara School of
Horticulture.

They secured a loan to begin KIVA. "The bank approved us
based on our business plan," says Kiera. "They saw a need in

the marketplace for our business—the design-build aspect sets us apart." The bank also recognized the calibre of the work that KIVA was offering, enhanced by the design awards Doug has won throughout his career such as the Trillium Award from the the city of St. Catharines.

The couple started small to help keep the amount of the loan down. For instance, the business is currently run from their home rather than outside offices. They needed the loan primarily for equipment—including a bobcat and some trucks—which were items that could be returned or resold if the business faltered.

Kiera is quick to stress the importance of a solid business plan in obtaining financing. She also advises other business owners: "Use your mentors. And contact your bank's small business department. Our bank manager was so helpful, and our mentors helped immensely with our business plan." Visit the company's website at **www.kivalandscape.com**.

Most businesses operate with a simple model. While the challenges and opportunities that have an impact on businesses may be complex, put simply, businesses create products or services to sell, generating a profit for their owners. The process of creating products and services requires resources, including capital.

Capital, the fuel of the enterprise, can be human and intellectual, but in almost every case it is also financial. Financial capital falls into two primary categories:

- **Debt:** money owed by a business, usually with specific terms of repayment, which is often referred to as a loan; and

- **Equity:** created by ownership of the business, such as when common shares are issued.

Either can be a mechanism a business uses to raise money to finance the acquisition of assets and to fund the business's day-to-day operation. Both types of capital have different characteristics that need to be considered when making decisions about the right way to fund the company's growth.

Successful small business owners choose capital structures that support their business objectives. They effectively balance debt and equity. When they take on debt it is structured for a specific use such as financing a piece of equipment or financing short-term cash flow until accounts receivable are paid, or inventory is sold. Alternately, equity provides a broader capital foundation that is available to fund a wide variety of business activities.

Thriving businesses ensure there is an appropriate amount of equity in the business, especially during periods of expansion. We can learn from the recent and numerous examples of large corporations that rapidly grew without having adequate equity in the business. Many funded their growth by aggressively borrowing. As a weaker economic environment developed, they could no longer support the debt; as a result, their whole business was endangered. An appropriate balance of debt and equity stabilizes the business. To determine what is appropriate for your business, let's further explore how financial capital is used and managed.

THE PROCESS OF FINANCIAL MANAGEMENT

Acquiring financial capital, ensuring it is effectively put to work in your business, and returning it to those who originally provided it is commonly referred to as the process of financial management. When it works efficiently, it not only achieves the objectives of the business owner but also meets the expectations of those who provided the capital in the first place.

Financial management generally refers to all aspects of the process of managing the business's financial resources. It incorporates financial planning, acquisition of capital, and cost control. Cost control and financial planning are topics covered in Chapters 4 and 5 in this book This chapter focuses more specifically on the process of acquiring capital.

By understanding the advantages and disadvantages of various types of capital that may be available to you—and by building effective systems to manage those financial resources—you can increase the growth potential in your small business. By planning appropriate capital structures, you will reduce the likelihood your business will be constrained by inadequate financial resources and restricted access to capital.

Capital Categories and Ownership Structure

When a business decides to raise capital it enters into a contract whereby it agrees to grant "consideration" to the provider of the capital. In the case of debt, consideration is usually in the form of interest paid to the lender above and beyond the original amount borrowed.

In the case of equity, the equity owner's consideration is generally in two forms:

1. through participation in the control of the company. In the case of a common shareholder this would be through voting rights.
2. by receiving a portion of the earnings of the company. In the case of a common shareholder these, earnings can be reinvested in the company as retained earnings or paid to the owners as dividends.

The legal structure of the business will determine what category of capital is potentially available to fund the business. Sole proprietors, partnerships, and incorporated businesses each have different options:

Sole Proprietors
These businesses often draw from personal financial resources to augment business loans that may be granted to the proprietorship. They may not need or wish to give up control of their business by involving partners, or shareholders.

Partnerships
Multiple individuals contribute personal financial resources to the business and will also likely have a say in how the business operates.

Incorporated Businesses
There are numerous possibilities as to how they can raise capital and a variety of sources from which it can be aquired.

A FEW WORDS FOR START-UPS

When starting a business, choosing the right ownership structure is a key decision you will have to make. The issues are:

- cost to incorporate, including additional ongoing administrative costs;
- the need to limit personal liability;
- gaining access to some types of capital; and
- tax considerations.

Work with advisers who will review your business plan and recommend appropriate structures that are right for your enterprise.

IMPLICATIONS FOR EXISTING BUSINESSES

For established business owners, as your business evolves or as your circumstances change, you may wish to reconsider your ownership structure.

Incorporated businesses are distinct legal entities from their owner(s), therefore you may consider incorporation when:

- liability issues become more complex;
- you need new tax-minimization strategies;
- you need to gain access to new capital sources; and
- you make structural changes that facilitate ownership transfer in succession or sale situations.

Innovation Image Inc.

In 2005, Perry Floreani and Annette Remboulis purchased Innovation Image from Perry's father, who had been running the small printing company since 1979. They've expanded it, creating a graphic arts and printing firm that specializes in boxes for food and pharmaceutical companies.

The company, located in Dorval, Quebec, has made the choice to outsource various aspects of its production and distribution processes to keep costs down. The couple purchase the cardboard and do the printing, but send the printed materials to a finisher, which completes the process of cutting and packing it, and a shipping company that transports the final product.

They've acquired financing through a variety of means. They initially secured a start-up loan from the Business Development Bank of Canada (BDC). Their personal experience—Perry had spent years in the printing business and Annette had started up businesses around the world—helped them secure the funding. When they needed a printing press, they went to a chartered bank and secured a government-guaranteed loan.

They ran into some financial trouble in the first year when the press they purchased was supposed to be assembled in four weeks and it took twelve. They sought help from financing consultants. "They were great," says Annette. "They found us a lending company that offered us a receivable loan to cover costs in the short term."

They have also used consultants to aid them in using the federal government's SR&ED (Scientific Research and Experimental Development) program—a tax credit incentive program that encourages Canadian companies to recover expenses related to research and development.

CHARACTERISTICS OF DEBT AND EQUITY

The two categories of capital have different attributes, making one alternative a good choice in some circumstances and a poor choice in others. Understanding these differences is important. Choosing the wrong type of capital can be like picking the wrong car. It looks great when you first get it, but over time it becomes clear it does not do what you wanted it to, and by the time you discover its limitations, it can be difficult to get rid of!

The attributes of financial capital have been categorized in the table on page 109.

Attributes of Types of Capital

	Debt	Equity
Costs	• Costs are in the form of interest. They will vary depending on the perceived level of risk and the type of lending vehicle. • There may be additional fees, such as application fees or monthly or annual administration fees. • These costs are reasonably predictable.	• Costs are in a share of the earnings. They will also depend on level of risk and type of equity.
Control	• The lender has limited to no control.	• Various levels of control are given to the capital provider, usually by being granted a vote at the board level. • Control is negotiated between the business and the capital provider.
Repayment Terms	• There are specific repayment terms for interest, or principal, or both. Negotiated in the original agreement (i.e., interest rate). It may be subject to periodic revision.	• There may be mechanisms to prescribe how equity may be redeemed, when, and for what consideration.
Default Remedies	• Debt providers have various rights to protect their interests when they lend to a business. The remedies to recover their capital will be set out in the loan agreement and are also established by law. • Collateral is often pledged in support of a loan, giving the lender the option to redeem the collateral to satisfy the debt in the event of default.	• Equity providers will have various rights to protect their interests in the capital they provide to a business. Again, these remedies to recover their capital will be set out in the original agreement and are also established by law.

CHOOSING BETWEEN DEBT AND EQUITY

Conceptually, the best capital in most small businesses is the owner's investment because in that case the investor's and owner's goals and objectives are one and the same.

Realistically, most businesses must reach out to external sources of capital to obtain enough cash to run the business. This introduces the need for the business owner to understand the objectives of the capital owner, and to factor those expectations into the day-to-day operation of the business.

Different categories of capital have different demands on the business. In most cases, debt will require regular payments of interest and principal, but the business owner does not give up any voting control and, therefore, is largely free to make decisions without the influence of capital owners.

On the other hand, equity may not have the same demands for regular payments as there is an option to modify dividends based on performance of the business. However, equity owners will normally require an element of control, which gives them the ability to safeguard their investment by influencing decisions that will affect their rate of return.

Making the choice between debt and equity requires an analysis of your cash flow and consideration of the degree to which you are prepared to give up control. In assessing their capital needs, most small business owners typically look first to the amount of personal investment they can commit to, keeping debt-servicing costs as low as possible while maintaining the highest level of control of their business.

DEBT

When considering debt financing and its availability, the business plan and cash-flow projections are particularly important. They:

- identify what levels of debt are sustainable by projecting the levels of cash flow required to meet repayment obligations;
- allow the business owner to consider various strategic plans and the revenue generated from different initiatives, as well as debt and/or equity required to support each initiative (each option can be modelled to evaluate a range of choices and the appropriateness of debt and equity combinations); and
- enable the business owner to demonstrate anticipated outcomes to lenders as part of the credit application process.

It's also important to match the business purpose to the type of loan. For example, financing current assets such as accounts receivable or inventory, with loans that have a fixed payment structure, such as a term loan, can create a cash-flow mismatch. The payment structure of a term loan will see the loan principle reduced on a straight-line basis over a longer period of time. This would be poorly suited to fund inventory, for example, which will increase and decrease over shorter time frames. As a result you may end up borrowing—and paying interest on—more debt than you actually require. Similarly, financing a long-term asset such as a vehicle or property with a short-term instrument such as a line of credit may also create a cash-flow mismatch.

There are a wide variety of debt instruments available, including lines of credit, term loans, and leases. Each has its advantages and disadvantages. A comparison of the various types of debt can be found on the following pages.

Type of Debt: Operating Loans, Lines of Credit

Purpose

It provides short-term financing to cover operating costs during the time it takes to collect current assets, such as receivables and inventory.

Costs

Interest rates are negotiated as a part of the loan agreement. Other costs, including application, administration, and renewal fees may apply. Interest rates are generally variable, often established at a rate "over the prime lending rate." Costs vary according to lender and risk.

Control

The lender does not normally assume any control over the business.

Repayment

These loans are usually authorized up to a maximum available lending limit and can be advanced and repaid as the cash flow permits. Interest is calculated based on the daily amount outstanding on the loan, and generally charged to the borrower on a monthly basis. Repayment is relatively flexible.

Remedies

In the event of default, the lender is afforded various rights against collateral and potentially against other assets of the business owners based on the loan and collateral agreements and other legal remedies.

Type of Debt: Credit Cards

Purpose

They provide short-term financing, offering the convenience of a readily available credit facility accepted as an alternative to cash payment by most businesses.

Costs

Interest costs vary widely, being set out in the cardholder agreement. Most cards offer a "grace period" in which no interest is charged provided the outstanding balance is paid in full by the due date. Fees such as an annual fee may be applicable depending on the issuer and the type of card, often based on various features including rewards points, insurance coverage, or cash back.

Control

The lender does not assume any control over the business.

Repayment

The cardholder agreement will set out minimum monthly payments usually established as a percentage of the outstanding balance. Payments are generally required monthly. Repayment is relatively flexible.

Remedies

In the event of default, the lender is afforded various legal rights to recover the amount owing. In some cases, credit cards can be secured, giving the lender additional remedies against the collateral held.

Type of Debt: Term Loans

Purpose

They provides long-term financing to assist with the acquisition of long-term assets such as equipment.

Costs

Interest costs are negotiated as a part of the loan agreement. Other costs, including application, administration, and renewal fees, may apply. Interest rates can be fixed or variable. Costs vary according to lender and risk.

Control

The lender does not normally assume any control over the business. The business gives up little control.

Repayment

These loans are usually repayable in a series of regular payments that include both principal and interest over a specific period of time. Repayment terms are set out in the loan agreement.

Remedies

In the event of default, the lender is afforded various rights against collateral and potentially against other assets of the business owners based on the loan and collateral agreements and other legal remedies. The lender has significant remedies in the event of default.

Type of Debt: Leases

Purpose

Leases provide long-term funding to purchase the use of fixed assets, as opposed to obtaining outright ownership of those assets.

Costs

Interest costs are negotiated as a part of the original lease agreement. Other costs, including application, administration, and renewal fees may apply. Interest rates can be fixed or variable. Costs vary according to leaser, the type of asset and the risk.

Control

The leaser does not normally assume any control over the business.

Repayment

Leases are repayable in a series of regular payments that include both principal and interest, and often taxes, over a specific period of time. Repayment is set out in the lease agreement.

Remedies

In the event of default, the leaser will recover the asset that it is leasing and have various rights to enforce the collection of any payments that may be required by the lease agreement. The lender has significant remedies in the event of default.

Type of Debt: Supplier Credit

Purpose
Supplier credit provides direct funding from the suppliers of a variety of business assets, from inventory to computer equipment.

Costs
Costs vary widely depending on the type of asset being acquired, the degree to which the vendor uses the financing program as an enticement for a sale, and the credit risk of the borrower. Costs vary according to lender and risk.

Control
The lender does not normally assume any control over the business. The business gives up little control.

Repayment
Each supplier will have terms that will vary widely from vendor to vendor. Repayment terms are set out in the supplier agreement.

Remedies
The supplier agreement will govern the remedies available to the vendor, in combination with applicable laws. The suppliers' remedies will vary depending on the agreement.

GRI Simulations Inc.

Russ Pelley is the president of GRI Simulations, based in Mount Pearl, Newfoundland, which provides ocean mapping services for domestic and international customers, including governments and oil companies. The company has become a global leader in underwater simulation.

Russ and senior staff bought the company in 2003, and found it quite difficult to manage cash flow at first. Personal funds and credit cards were initially enough to squeeze them through. "A contract from the Canadian Navy helped us considerably," says Russ. Oil companies soon followed.

Now cash flow is less of an issue. They receive a down payment from most of their customers, and GRI follows up with an invoice with thirty-day payment terms.

Russ has brought his previous experience as a chartered accountant to the business. He also worked with a bank for two years, and so has an understanding of what banks expect.

"Don't spring surprises on your bank," he says. "Keep an open communication with your account manager. And don't ignore warning signals." Russ stresses that by doing so you can often find a solution to an impending problem before it becomes a crisis.

"Know your business and the cash-flow implications of various decisions," says Russ. "Pay close attention to your payroll, to managing your receivables. Then contact your local bank or the BDC if you need it." Visit the company's website at **www.grisim.com**.

EQUITY

Equity is the capital that owners invest in their businesses. It can be acquired in different ways. The first is from the profits generated by the business. This happens over time and is reflected on the balance sheet of the business as owners' equity or retained earnings, depending on the legal structure of the business. When business owners choose to leave profits in the business, they will increase the equity base available to fund operations, reducing the need to find other sources of capital.

The second way to acquire equity is to seek equity investors. Equity investments can be contributed by the owners or partners in a business or by external investors. Most equity investments include a mechanism whereby the investor is granted an element of control at either the board decision-making level or in some cases more actively in the day-to-day management of the business. Equity investers become owners.

Equity investors will want to have a clear picture of the business's plan to use their investment. They will usually want a full business plan with financial projections to support the request for funding. They will normally undertake a process of due diligence in which they will assess the owner's objectives, projections, and track record, as well as conduct an evaluation of management's ability to achieve the businesses objectives.

Generally equity investors will want to receive a rate of return on their investment that delivers a premium to deflect the risk they are assuming. Because equity investments are not normally supported by assignment of fixed assets as collateral, the investors' ability to "pick a winner" becomes even more critical.

There are two primary types of equity investments: common shares and preferred shares. Each has advantages and disadvantages. Here is a comparison, outlining their different attributes.

Type of Equity: Common Shares

Purpose

Common shares provide capital that becomes available to any of the activities of the business requiring cash flow.

Costs

Common shareholders are paid a dividend established by the business on a periodic basis. Costs vary according to dividends declared.

Control

Common shareholders will have voting control of the business, participating in the decision making of the company according to the share of ownership they have. The business gives up control in proportion to the percentage of ownership held by voting shareholders.

Repayment

The share's face value can be recovered when the shareholder redeems it, in which case the company returns the share's original face value to the investor. The terms governing when a share can be redeemed are established in the original agreement between the shareholder and the company, referred to as "the offer." Redemption options vary and are set out in the original stock offer.

Remedies

In the event of default, common shareholders are the last to be paid when a business winds up. While they have legal remedies, these are limited. Claims against the company are subordinate to debt and preferred shareholders.

Type of Equity: Preferred Shares

Purpose

Preferred shares provide capital that becomes available to any of the activities of the business requiring cash flow.

Costs

Preferred shareholders are paid a dividend established by the business on a periodic basis. These dividends are paid in priority to common shareholder dividends. Costs vary according to dividends declared.

Control

Preferred shareholders do not normally have voting control over the business. The business experiences no loss of control

Repayment

The share's face value can be recovered when the shareholder redeems it, in which case the company returns the share's original face value to the investor. The terms governing when a share can be redeemed are established in the original agreement between the shareholder and the company, referred to as "the offer." Redemption options vary and are set out in the original stock offer.

Remedies

In the event of default, preferred shareholders are paid after secured debt holders and before common shareholders. Claims are subordinated to secured debt holders.

SOURCES OF FINANCIAL CAPITAL

Different sources of capital will also have different character-istics. These are a result of differing expectations on the part of the capital owner. The source of capital is different from the type of capital; the source refers to the individual or insti-tution that provides the loan or equity.

Various sources can have distinctly different characteris-tics and expectations. For example, a loan from a friend will have different characteristics than a loan from a financial in-stitution. The terms of the loan (things like interest rate, pay-ments, or collateral requirements) may be exactly the same, but, practically speaking, the expectations of each source may be entirely different. You may see your friend every weekend and the topic of "how's business?" now takes on a new dimen-sion that can complicate the relationship. The friend may be willing to keep repayment arrangements informal, while a fi-nancial institution will have established policies that govern the options it can offer.

Sources of Debt Financing
Chartered Banks

- Offer a wide range of financing options, from credit cards to loans, leases, and mortgages.
- Governed by policies designed to make credit available to the largest group of potential customers, while protecting depositors through prudent lending practices.
- Often have business specialists who can assist you by pro-viding practical advice, access to tools and resources, and ongoing support for various financial strategies.

Business Development Bank of Canada

- In Canada, a federally mandated bank that provides lending services to fund loans that would not normally be considered by a chartered bank.
- These loans can be negotiated to complement chartered bank lending, or as a stand-alone financing alternative.

Credit Unions

- Offer many of the same products available through banks.
- Business services are part of a membership in the credit union.
- Policies are established by their respective boards, and loan applications are often adjudicated by a committee.

Friends and Family

- Particularly during the early phases of a business, many small business owners fund growth through private sources, including parents, siblings, and friends.

Shareholder Loans

- Shareholders will often inject capital into a business in the form of a loan.

Suppliers

- Suppliers of equipment or of your business inputs (such as inventory) may offer credit to facilitate the purchase of their goods.

Sources of Equity Financing
Private Investors

- Investors can range from family members to venture capitalists.
- Potential investors can be people you know through personal relationships, business networks, or business development organizations in your community.
- Angel investors are usually wealthy individuals who make equity investments in smaller enterprises.
- Venture capital sources typically fund larger, more complex transactions.
- The Internet can be helpful in identifying sources of investment.

Public Offerings

- For some businesses with sufficient size and resources, a formal public offering of shares can provide access to capital markets.

THE EFFECT OF RISK ON SOURCES OF CAPITAL

Risk is that dimension—present in every activity—that creates the possibility of unintended outcomes. In business, especially as it relates to financing, risk is a significant element when considering how a business will achieve its goals.

The question is not, "Is there any risk in this venture?" as there is at least some degree of risk in anything. Instead, the questions are: What are the risks? Are they being dealt with in such a way as to minimize their potential negative consequences?

Your business will have elements of risk by virtue of internal and external factors with the potential to derail your plans. A lender or investor who is considering a request to provide capital for your business will evaluate the degree of risk through a process that asks a series of questions such as:

- What are the key risk factors for this business?
- Have the business owners identified the risks appropriately?
- Is there a plan in place to minimize the negative consequences of the identified risk?
- Do the business and/or its owners have a track record of effectively dealing with risks?

To the degree you can answer these questions positively, lenders or investors will feel more comfortable working with your business. This comfort may be reflected in their willingness to make more capital available, grant better interest rates, attach fewer conditions or reporting requirements, or lower their requirements for control.

The good news is that most risk is manageable. Chapter 7 discusses risk-management processes in greater detail. Your track record in dealing with risk will be one of the key indicators a lender or investor will use to predict what they can expect of you and your business in the future.

WHAT FINANCIAL INSTITUTIONS LOOK FOR IN A LENDING APPLICATION

The process of applying for a loan with a financial institution, such as a bank or credit union, usually incorporates a formal application process. Before starting this process, it's useful to know what most institutions look for when they consider a credit application.

Good Credit History

This is a real, tangible reflection of your past success in dealing with risk factors. As such, it becomes a practical tool to predict your future ability to manage finances. Therefore, it is particularly important to protect your credit history—both personal and business. There is a general continuum to the importance of the owner's personal credit history. The small credit requests for say, a sole proprietor, are based largely on the individual doing the borrowing. The larger requests, or requests from larger businesses, tend to be based more on a combination of both the owner's personal situation and the business itself. At the high end of the range, requests for large corporations are entirely based on the business's ability to repay the debt. A credit bureau report will usually be obtained to gain a full picture of your credit history. In Canada, there are two main bureaus providing personal credit reports: Equifax and TransUnion. Both operate websites that provide descriptions on how credit reports are used and how to view your personal report. A lender will also assess the credit history of the business. Business credit bureaus include Dun & Bradstreet, and Equifax. It is good practice to periodically review your own credit reports to ensure their accuracy.

The Owner's Personal Investment or Equity in the Business

A personal investment demonstrates commitment—financial and otherwise—to the business. Equity from the owner(s) or from other sources, such as investors or retained earnings, also provides the business with more flexibility in dealing with unforeseen events. A lender or investor will want to see that the owner has demonstrated his or her commitment to the venture with the first injection of capital or by leaving enough equity in retained earnings to ensure the business's financial health.

The Ability of the Business to Repay the Loan

Will the business generate enough cash to repay the loan? For an existing business, this assessment is demonstrated by assessing the company's most recent financial statements, the business plan, and cash-flow projections. For new start-ups, the application will be supported by financial projections, including forecasts for the balance sheet, the income statements, and the cash-flow statements, each of which will be assessed to determine the likelihood that cash will be available to service financial obligations. The assessment will also focus on the degree to which known market factors such as industry trends, the competitive environment, and the owner's experience, skills, and abilities assure the lender that the loan will be repaid as agreed.

Collateral

In the event of default of the loan, collateral helps to protect the lender. This collateral can be the equipment or property that is being financed by the loan, or some other asset. The personal assets of the business owner may also be pledged in support of business loans. Collateral will rarely be the sole reason for granting a loan, but is an alternate source of repayment.

If an application is declined, it is likely because one or a combination of these elements are absent. If your business has been turned down for credit, it is important to find out why. Is it a problem you can fix? For example, if the initial assessment suggests the business will not generate enough cash to repay to loan, can business plans be adjusted accordingly? It is always difficult to hear that a loan request has been declined, but many business owners point out this is the time when a good lender really earns its keep. Be sure to get the lender's insights as to why the application was not approved. Lenders can provide critical information about your business plans and even identify alternatives, such as government lending programs. They can highlight opportunities to improve your business plan and mitigate risks that may have contributed to the negative response.

WORKING WITH ADVISERS

The process of raising capital to fund a business venture can be a complicated one. It's complex not only from the perspective of knowing how to identify the right type and source of capital, but also by virtue of the slew of tax and legal considerations relevant to many decisions a business owner must make.

Those who have worked to find the right balance of debt and equity emphasize the importance of obtaining appropriate advice and information to guide decision making. Good advice helps avoid potential pitfalls. Many businesses have encountered setbacks because debt-to-equity levels were unmanageable. Surrounding yourself with advisers whom you are comfortable with, who have the required level of expertise, and who will be available when you need them, will pay dividends by contributing to both the short- and long-term success of your business.

UNLOCKING KEY: Consider which sources of capital are right for your business and test their effects on your financial projections by using the "what if" capabilities of business-planning tools.

Get Growing *for business* Online Resource: A Capital-Planning worksheet helps you identify and systematically review capital ownership options for your business, preparing you to incorporate the right choices into your business plan (**www.getgrowingforbusiness.com/unlocking/finances**).

KEEPING CONTROL OF YOUR FINANCES

Using practical day-to-day financial management systems can help an owner manage and control the business's financial position. We've covered four key financial areas to target when seeking to optimize financial results:

- generating revenue;
- cash flow;
- cost control; and
- capital structure.

These systems become valuable management tools to help you monitor your results, save time and money, and identify critical issues, such as a looming cash shortfall, before they manifest themselves as a major crisis. Here are some approaches that have been particularly helpful to many businesses.

Accounting Software

Accounting software programs simplify financial processes such as tracking revenue and expenses, monitoring actual results against established budgets and organizing financial record keeping. For example, Intuit QuickBooks®* offers software specifically tailored to the needs of small business owners as well as a network of bookkeepers and accountants certified as "QuickBooks ProAdvisors," who are also experts in the use of this software.

Online Banking

Online banking gives you easy access to both business and

personal banking information when and where you need it. It allows you to monitor balances and complete transactions conveniently. Whether paying business taxes or other bills, transferring money between accounts, or getting access to planning tools and resources, online banking can reduce your costs while giving you a management tool that makes accurate and timely information readily available.

Cash-Management Strategies

Electronic cash-management products further enhance your ability to manage your finances and accelerate cash flow. These solutions will differ from one financial institution to another. Work with your small business adviser to identify which approach is best suited to your business needs.

Advanced Online Banking Solutions

Similar to online banking, these programs offer incremental cash management capabilities such as customizable functionality, which grants trusted employees or advisers the ability to monitor and manage accounts using assigned user privileges. For example, consider a bookkeeper who might be granted privileges to create a payment transaction (such as payroll or bill payments) while authority to approve and execute those transactions would be still be retained by the business owner.

Electronic Funds Transfer (EFT)

These payment services can be set up to automate both the outgoing and incoming payments of a business. The result is significantly improved control over cash flow and reduced costs associated with payment and receivable administration. For example, consider a contractor who drives to each job site every second Friday to pay employees by cheque. By automating these payments directly to the employees' bank accounts, travel is reduced, as are the costs to prepare, handle, and reconcile each cheque that is issued. Similarly, for incoming payments, consider a lawn-care business that invoices customers each time their lawn is attended to. By automating these receivables and setting up pre-authorized payments under a "subscription plan," the business will eliminate the time and expense associated with two labour-intensive processes: creating and mailing paper invoices and receiving and depositing the cheques once the customer ultimately pays.

Wire Payments

These can help you deliver high value and time-sensitive payments to your key business partners in Canada or worldwide. They typically replace cheques, money orders, and courier services while reducing the risk of fraud, and save you time by eliminating the need to contact or visit your branch. You can send payments in Canadian or foreign currency to most major financial institutions around the world. Numerous additional features simplify the administration of these payments and enhance the security of these transactions.

6

HUMAN RESOURCES MANAGEMENT

Hannigan Honey Inc.

Albert Hannigan began producing honey during World War II when sugar was being rationed. He started with two beehives he purchased from the Eaton's catalogue. Today Hannigan Honey is run by Albert's son, Murray, and the company manages 4,000 hives.

Murray is quick to attribute a good part of his success to the people who surround him. "I have acquired and retained very good staff," he says. "Our largest expense is labour, and finding good people is critical." This is particularly true for their company, as finding experienced beekeepers is not an easy task.

The workload is seasonal, with work ramping up in April and finishing in November. They have some students who work in the winter, doing maintenance on the hives and other off-season tasks. "In the summer we have about twenty-eight people on the payroll," says Murray. "It cuts back to about eight in the winter."

Murray takes measures to ensure he can retain his uniquely qualified staff. During the off-season, he tops up their Employment Insurance (EI) earnings so they're still getting 90 per cent of their pay.

Murray's approach to his people is, "Assume your employees mean to do right. If there's a failure somewhere, look to what went wrong and communicate about it. That's how my father treated me," he says. "Also, have confidence in your employees and give them more responsibility. Most are anxious to prove themselves."

Throughout our cross-country tour, we met hundreds of entrepreneurs who rose daily to meet the challenges and capitalize on the opportunities they created. Their passion was contagious. They were excited by the future possibilities of their business. They were aware of the challenges and they were attacking them head on.

We were constantly reminded of a simple fact: small business owners wear many hats. Most small businesses simply don't have the grand scale needed to hire the experts you often find in larger organizations. In areas such as human resources, they have to either rely on external support or do it themselves. Most often, they use a combination of both. Finding the right mix of internal and external resources depends to a large degree on the type of issues a business faces, the internal resources available, and an assessment of the potential impact of staffing alternatives on bottom-line performance.

Small businesses are built on people. In some of the businesses we encountered, the key resource was one person: the owner. In other cases, larger groups of talented individuals contributed their respective skills and abilities. No matter what the mix, human resources are clearly a critical element in the process of unlocking a business's growth potential. They warrant particular attention because this can be a key area with an impact on the bottom line. Here are some of the key aspects of human resources management we saw in successful small businesses.

YOU: THE SMALL BUSINESS OWNER

Let's start by taking care of you!

Running a small business offers you the opportunity to be your own boss, the promise of financial success, and the chance to creatively develop your unique product or service in new and exciting ways. But, as with most things in life, there are two sides to every coin: the opportunity and the challenge. When running a small business, you'll experience a variety of both. Here are just a few:

Opportunity: To be your own boss.
Challenge: Being an effective manager and using your skills and abilities to achieve your business goals.

Opportunity: To exercise creative control.
Challenge: Bearing the responsibility for the ultimate success of what you create.

Opportunity: Financial success.

Challenge: Generating profits by effectively executing strategies that impact sales and marketing, cash flow, costs, revenue, human resources, and dealing with the risk of losses.

Clearly, being a small business owner is a demanding role.

HAVING FUN

As one owner put it, "If I'm not having fun any more, I'd better stop doing it." In many ways the reality of a fast-paced, creatively stimulating, relationship-oriented role is the very thing that brings joy to an entrepreneur.

It's important to occasionally sit back and remind yourself of the original reasons you went into business. Ask yourself: "Am I in this business for the same reasons I was originally? Am I still gaining personal satisfaction from this? If not, what's changed?"

Next, identify the aspects of your business you enjoy, and those you dread. Make a list. Write them down.

UNLOCKING KEY: Deliberately revisit the reasons you originally went into business and make a point of re-evaluating them periodically. This will help you understand if, and why, they may have changed. Next write down those aspects of running your business that you enjoy and those you dread.

Creating this list allows you to look at things two ways. For those aspects you enjoy, find ways to do them more often. At the very least, you can consciously recognize them when they occur. For those things you dread, is there a way to eliminate or reduce the time you spend on them? Can you delegate these activities? How about outsourcing certain practices? Could you even alter a product or service you offer?

Working to keep the fun in business helps you stay energized and effective. Reducing the amount of time you spend on things that leave you feeling emotionally taxed or out of your comfort zone will contribute to a stronger sense of personal fulfillment. You cannot eliminate all of the things you find difficult, but, as with everything else in business, you can take steps to manage them.

We met some entrepreneurs who loved to sell and market, but hated the administrative or operational aspects of their role as a business owner. Conversely, we met others that had the opposite likes and dislikes. In ideal situations, these types of individuals worked together with partners in business, complementing each others' strengths. Partnership may not be the best choice for you, but perhaps there is an existing employee who has the skills you do not have, or one who would like the opportunity to develop through a targeted training initiative.

NURTURING SKILLS AND ABILITIES

Because there are so many dimensions to running a successful business, it's important for entrepreneurs like you to identify your strengths and weaknesses. It helps you make decisions regarding those elements you will take personal responsibility for, and which ones you should delegate or outsource.

On our tour, we did not meet any entrepreneurs who professed to be great at everything. We met some amazing people who came close, but even they saw the opportunity to achieve better results by recognizing their own limitations. Then they created training strategies to improve their abilities or found people who could do the jobs more effectively.

UNLOCKING KEY: Complete a skills and abilities evaluation to identify your areas of strength, areas for development, and aspects of your business that you can more effectively accomplish by delegating or outsourcing.

LIFE BALANCE

Small business owners are often defined by what they do. They are so immersed in their enterprise that their personal life and business life meld together. It can be difficult to find a good balance. Yet, on the other hand, entrepreneurship provides unique alternatives for a lifestyle that might not be available through a traditional job with an employer.

The first step for the entrepreneur is to define what he or she means by "balance." It's different for everyone. Establish some specific goals in terms of what your ideal life balance might look like. Is it measured by how you allocate time between running the business and activities with family and friends? Or is it based on other goals, such as making a contribution to your community or achieving other social objectives that are important to you? Does balance have more to do with personal, financial, social, or spiritual fulfillment? It's often some combination of many factors.

This lifestyle "balance sheet" often has many dimensions. Set aside time to consciously decide what is important to you. Once you've decided on the details, write them down and make sure you keep them in mind as you create business and personal plans.

Now identify those aspects of your business that run contrary to your goals. A pitfall that many owners we spoke with encountered was the risk of devoting too much time to the business and neglecting other aspects of their lives. For many owners, it became impossible to sustain other important dimensions of their lives and find a balance. To paraphrase marketing author Michael Hepworth, time is the one commodity we all have in common: twenty-four hours in a day to use any way we choose. What we can control are the choices we make.

Once you're clear on your priorities, you can begin to identify those day-to-day activities that do not contribute to your goals, and begin to eliminate them. By choosing to focus on high-return activities and eliminating the rest, you can dramatically improve efficiency, and free up time for other priorities. It may mean you "fire" low-return or high-maintenance customers, or don't reply to non-critical emails. Remember that you do have choices to restore balance while maintaining (or even improving) profitability.

Good human resources management strategies begin with effective management of your most important success factor: you!

> **Get Growing** *for business* **Online Resource:** The Human Resources Self-Assessment worksheet helps you revisit the reasons you went into business, the aspects of business ownership that you enjoy, and those you don't. It asks what balance looks like for you, and leads you through a process to create an inventory of your strengths and weaknesses. Finally, it helps you re-establish personal priorities, letting you modify those aspects of your business that are not matched to your priorities. The goal is to work toward keeping the fun in owning your own business (**www.getgrowingforbusiness.com/unlocking/hr**).

Center City Tire & Auto

We met Jeff Roberts in Chapter 1 and learned about the growth of his Alberta-based automotive service businesses. With about twenty-five people on his staff, human resources is obviously an important aspect of his enterprise.

"I hire people, not credentials," says Jeff. "There are things you can teach and things you can't." Jeff personally interviews potential new employees in a process that usually lasts anywhere from one-and-a-half to two hours. "Our business is about relationship building, so you need team players. It's important."

He realizes the importance of long-term planning when it comes to hiring. While it may be easier in the short term to quickly hire a needed replacement person, Jeff feels it's far more important to wait it out until he finds the right candidate. "I'd rather have a vacant position than hire the wrong person," he says.

Jeff stresses the importance of having an employee handbook that contains job descriptions, rates of pay, and policies like cellphone use and break times. "We have terrible memories—people do," he says. "A new staff member can't just be told something; it needs to be written down."

"Manage your people," Jeff suggests. "They're your biggest asset and without them you have nothing."

THE CARE AND MAINTENANCE OF YOUR TEAM

As a small business grows, it reaches a point where it must begin to rely on a group of individuals to deliver its product or service. That team may initially be made up of part-time employees or outsourced service providers, eventually growing to include full-time staff as well. The best enterprises create an environment in which each of these individuals understands and contributes to the broader objectives of the business. They need to be aware of—and work toward—the "big picture."

As you progress from being an owner-operator to the manager of a business team, the focus on facilitating the group's ability to consistently deliver excellence becomes one of the most important aspects of building short- and long-term success. While specific approaches vary, we have seen some key attributes appear consistently in the most successful enterprises.

Clearly Communicated Vision

When it was just you running your business and you were the only employee, you could say with confidence that all employees clearly understood the vision and objectives of the business. It's easy to accomplish when you're a team of one! A fundamental shift occurs when the team expands. The owner must share his or her vision and objectives and, even more importantly, the other team members must understand and adopt them as their own. It's no different for partnerships, with the added twist that partners must be certain they agree on vision and objectives to be effective. Success comes down to fostering a work environment with open two-way communication. Here are some tried-and-true communication strategies:

- Write your vision for the business in the form of a mission statement and a value proposition (see below).
- Incorporate both the mission statement and value proposition into the fabric of your business on a day-to-day basis. Refer to them during staff meetings, post them on the wall, and refer to them in your conversations. Reference how your decisions support them. This will help your staff when they are making decisions of their own.
- Work to build a trusting, open work environment where people's opinions are respected and criticism is withheld, unless it is constructive and in the right forum.
- Create a staff bulletin board, write a newsletter, hold strategy sessions, or offer a suggestion box—anything that opens up avenues to exchange information.

Definitions

Mission statement: A formal summary of the intentions and values of the company.

Value proposition: A concise statement that summarizes why a customer should buy your company's product or service.

Create an Inclusive Environment

When your staff believe their contribution is valued by the team, they are more willing to adopt the objectives of the group as their own. In essence, it creates a team atmosphere.

- Create a non-threatening environment where staff are able to identify obstacles to achieving business goals.
- Demonstrate your willingness to incorporate changes arising from staff suggestions, highlighting the value you receive from this input.
- Follow up in a specific amount of time—say a month or two—to see how the suggestion worked out.

Clearly Define Expectations

When members of your team know exactly what is expected of them, who has the authority to make what decisions, and where to go when things go wrong, you will dramatically increase their level of satisfaction. Higher satisfaction then translates into better performance. You need to have in place a few non-negotiable items so that your staff are clear on expectations.

- An organizational chart defining who reports to whom.
- A clear chain of command, letting people know whom they should address problems to, and what to do in a case in which their immediate supervisor may be part of the problem.
- Detailed job descriptions that outline an individual's day-to-day responsibilities and the levels of authority you have delegated to that person.
- Policies for the workplace, including lunch and break times, personal phone calls, email and computer use, and so on.

Celebrate Team and Individual Success

When a team has a common goal, achieving that goal re-affirms both the value of the team and the individual contri-bution of each member of that team. Make a big deal of successes by consciously and intentionally celebrating signifi-cant milestones.

- Use formal programs such as employee-of-the-month awards programs or performance certificates to celebrate special contributions.
- Find opportunities to express your personal appreciation.
- Create events to recognize when an employee reaches par-ticularly significant milestones, like exceeding a monthly sales objective, a promotion, or a certain number of years with the company.

There is no better strategy than to have a genuine interest in the well-being of your team. No mission statement or rec-ognition program will replace your ability to build strong, trusting relationships with the people who work for you. Take the time to deliberately consider how successful you have been in creating a workplace where your team feels included and valued.

Talk with your employees. Be attentive to both what they say, as well as non-verbal cues in their body language that let you know how you're doing and where you need to focus your attention. It is often helpful to engage the services of external advisers who can help you gain an insight into how successful you and your management team have been in identifying staff and employee issues. Getting it right will pay off in a variety of ways, including higher efficiency, a lower staff turnover rate, and a positive environment for your staff—and you!

PICKING THE RIGHT PEOPLE FOR YOUR BUSINESS

You'll get a head start on creating a positive working environment by picking the right employees to join your team. Yet finding the right fit can be a difficult task. It is made even more challenging when there is a shortage of qualified people in the marketplace.

Generally, the most successful recruiters we met were business owners who had thought about their company and the jobs that needed to be filled from the candidate's perspective. They answered the question that good candidates ask themselves. "Why would I want to work for you and your business?"

Some business owners highlighted the work environment—for example, that it was in a great location, was steadily busy but not stressful; other like-minded people work there; and so on. Others outlined the opportunities to gain experience, whether through learning new computer programs, gaining a set of valuable skills, or working in a job that was an extension of something the candidate already knew how to do. These owners were able to differentiate their business by highlighting the positive aspects of their business and, as a result, found recruiting easier than those who simply provide job titles and contact information.

Here are some additional approaches we've seen that increase the likelihood of finding the right people to work in your business.

- Think long term. Identify the skills you'll need from your new employees now—and in the future—relative to your key goals for the company.
- Identify the specific characteristics you are looking for in a new employee. Then identify the skills you'll need. An individual's personality is not likely to change much, so you are better off hiring someone with the traits you're looking for even if he or she doesn't have the experience. After all, you can train new skills, but you can't teach people to be who they're not.
- In tight labour markets, you may have to be flexible on what you require. While you need to be clear on the minimum traits and skills that you need from your new employee, remain flexible on things you can teach or coach over time.
- Make sure you have the job description clearly laid out. You'll need it when you interview new candidates and it can be a valuable aid in discussing candidate strengths and weaknesses.
- One key source of new employees is existing employees. Ask your existing workforce if they know anyone who would be a good potential applicant for the job. Depending on the nature of your business, this is often an excellent initial recruiting method, because it can spare you the cost and time of placing a job ad, sorting through resumés, and doing countless interviews.
- Before you advertise, ask yourself if you really need to hire a new person. Perhaps you would do better by retraining someone who is already a member of your team. You may still have to hire to replace that person, but it may be easier to find candidates who qualify for an entry-level position,

and you'll get the additional strength of a seasoned employee in a more senior position.

- When you do advertise the available position, be clear and specific about what you are looking for. Include the title of the position, what the job entails, and what the offered salary or hourly rate is. Also be specific about how candidates should contact you—by phone or by sending a resumé by fax or email.
- Think outside the box. Look into programs that help new Canadians find work, or co-op programs through schools.
- Before you hire, do a full background check. Call the references and previous employers whom your interviewees provide. It's much easier to avoid a hiring error before offering a position than after.

Where to Advertise

There are a variety of places to post your job ad. It's important to consider the type of employee you're looking for, as different methods of advertising target different types of employees.

Online job boards: This is an increasingly viable way to find employees, especially if you're looking for a computer-savvy or young workforce, as they generally live on the Web. Plus, on some of the simpler classified boards, they have the added bonus of being free!

Newspaper: This traditional method of advertising still works well. Costs vary depending on where you live, the size of the paper, and how long you run the ad. Many newspapers have now teamed with online job sites to put your classified listing on the Internet as well.

College and university postings: Current students as well as alumni make use of the job boards available at their college or university. This is a great way to find seasonal staff, as well as people who have been trained in the discipline you're looking for. It is typically a low-cost or even no-cost way to find staff.

Government job boards: The federal and provincial governments have their own boards where you can post a vacant position—typically for free. They are also a good resource for finding subsidy programs for hiring and training.

Specialized job boards: Many professional and trade associations offer job postings at their location or on their websites related to a specific discipline (for example, engineering). These postings may be free to anyone or available only through membership to the organization.

MANAGING THE WORK

The owners of growing companies will face new staffing demands simply by virtue of the increasing size of their operation. In addition, there is the increased complexity of the processes that exist in larger businesses.

Obviously it takes a different set of skills to complete a given task yourself as opposed to having an employee take responsibility for it. When you're on your own, you do all the work yourself. As a manager, you are presented with the task of managing a team who will get things done on your behalf. As a company grows in size, the success of the business begins to rely more and more on the ability of others to effectively complete the tasks, and the owner's abilities as an effective manager.

Managing work by managing others becomes easier when you do the following:

- Break every process down into its individual tasks. Write down each task and create a formal workflow.
- Clearly identify who is responsible for each task within those workflows. Then incorporate each task into position descriptions for all the employees in your business. Having a written job description makes job responsibilities clear to your existing staff. It also makes your job easier if you need to hire a replacement person for a vacant position.
- Establish clear measures of success for each position. These could be in terms of production output (e.g., producing 100 widgets a day), sales results (e.g., bringing in $50,000 of new business a month), customer satisfaction (leading to repeat business), or other measurable indicators that work for your business.
- Create a framework to provide regular performance feedback to staff. You should let them know about their individual results, as well as relate their contribution to the broader performance of the business.
- Recognize individual contribution through formal performance reviews; however, don't neglect to take advantage of the informal feedback opportunities that occur every day. These allow your employees to see how well they're performing their tasks right when, or immediately after, they've performed them.
- Consider how to improve your team's productivity. Is there technology or equipment available to streamline

tasks and make your team more effective? Can you out-source non-core functions to enable your staff to have a better focus?

- Identify opportunities for coaching and training in order to keep employees up to date with current practices, or to upgrade their skills and abilities. These might be computer classes, training sessions for new product lines, team-building exercises, or even a presentation by a motivational speaker.
- Ask your staff for suggestions about improvements to in-crease the efficiency or effectiveness of any of the processes.

COMPENSATION AND REWARDS

There are many theories about why people work—and money is not the only factor. People have different motivations, and what engages one person will not necessarily motivate another.

As we toured various businesses, we met some of the hun-dreds of thousands of people employed by Canadian small businesses, from production-floor labourers to front-office customer service personnel. It was not hard to identify those who love their jobs and those who are simply earning a paycheque. Depending on the role they play in each business, that difference in attitude has the potential to be a key success factor—or it can really hold the business back.

If achieving high employee morale were as simple as pay-ing everyone a lot of money, this chapter on Human Re-sources Management would be much shorter. We met some highly paid employees who were not very happy people, and some happy minimum-wage earners making outstanding contributions.

Nevertheless, the role of compensation needs to be understood in its rightful place—among a number of factors that keep your staff firing on all cylinders.

Remember, when it comes to creating happy, positive employees: "Money will not buy you happiness"—although it can help. Here are some ideas to consider:

- Create an environment where you reward outstanding results. Your staff should know that going above and beyond what's expected of them will be recognized.
- Establish a compensation framework that is clearly understood by your staff. Highlight not only wages and salary, but also other benefits that are a part of the compensation program, such as vacations, insurance coverage, or group RSP programs.
- Consider establishing a merit program that is tied to your performance management program, creating systematic monetary increases to recognize performance achievement.
- Make sure your wages and salaries are competitive in your specific market.
- Create special recognition programs that are specifically not monetary in nature, from employee-of-the-month designations to recognition letters.

When you create an environment in which people feel their contribution is valued, recognized, and respected, a solid compensation and rewards program will be the icing on the cake. Relying on wages and salaries alone will be expensive and ineffective in the long run. Finding that right mix of compensation, rewards, and recognition will help you create and sustain your business's competitive advantage.

Get Growing *for business* Online Resource: The Human Resources Staff Management worksheet provides a checklist designed to assist you in establishing processes and programs that support high employee-satisfaction levels, an efficient workforce, and high staff morale (www.getgrowingforbusiness.com/unlocking/hr).

EnviroSeal Engineering Products Ltd.

EnviroSeal Engineering was incorporated in 1980 in Bedford, Nova Scotia, by husband and wife partners Joseph and Aniko Dunford. Initially, EnviroSeal was a marketing company for specialized equipment serving heavy industries like pulp and paper, chemical processing, and mining. Over the years, Joseph realized there was a need in the fluid-sealing product offering. As a result, he created new inventions that revolutionized the pumping industry.

Joseph passed away in 1999 and Aniko is now the sole owner of the business. "We refocused the company to solely manufacture our inventions over the last fourteen years," says Aniko. "Our products are patented worldwide."

Aniko leads a staff of twenty-two who are responsible for a variety of jobs, including manufacturing, administration, technical support, training, and research.

"The approach we have in house for HR," says Aniko, "is to

simply advance our own people whenever possible, rather than hire from outside. Over the years a total of five machinists have advanced to technical support/sales positions. Aside from this, my approach is that I compensate them extremely well, but expect extremely high performance. The systems and philosophy we have in place have proven to be very effective, productive, and satisfying over the years."

The philosophy at EnviroSeal is working. "Our turnover rate in twenty-nine years is less than 1 per cent." Visit the company's website at **www.enviroseal.ca**.

WHEN AN EMPLOYEE IS JUST NOT WORKING OUT

Many of the small business owners we met felt like their staff was essentially an extended family. So in situations where things were just not working out with an employee, these entrepreneurs faced a unique challenge. It was clear that this can be one of the most difficult aspects of running a small business.

On the one hand, business owners trust their employees with various aspects of the business. They expect their employees to be an extension of themselves to some degree, reflecting their passion, striving to achieve their standard of excellence, and protecting their reputation for the long-term benefit of the business.

On the other hand, when you ask an employee to undertake a given task, he or she expects support in an environment where he or she can achieve success. Success is different for different people. It may be a desire to achieve a sense of stability, personal satisfaction, or financial rewards.

When either party is dissatisfied it's important to address the situation quickly and effectively in order to minimize any consequences to the business.

Here are some approaches that helped many of the business owners we talked to:

- Be proactive about creating an open workplace where staff feel free to discuss problems when they are small—before they get out of hand.
- Deliberately communicate your expectations. With job descriptions, ensure they're written down and accessible to your employees. If you're assigning a specific task, provide specific instructions and a timeline. Also remind staff regularly of broader objectives—the "big picture"—like achieving specific quality or service standards by reaffirming the company's mission statement and value propositions.
- Be clear when your expectations are not met. Don't give a generalized criticism of an employee's performance. Provide specific examples. Define what you see as acceptable standards of performance. Outline your specific expectations in terms of measurable results.
- Establish reasonable time frames to accomplish the required level of performance. Depending on the type of change, it could be revisited in a week, a month, or three months. In the interim, provide any necessary support to your employee to enable him or her to achieve the expected performance outcomes.

If all else fails and you feel you have no choice but to fire the employee, be aware of the legal implications of your actions. If needed, seek professional advice to minimize your exposure to legal action based on wrongful dismissal. Also be sure to contact the provincial and federal governments regarding labour standards and requirements, including the necessary paperwork you will have to file.

Be aware of your rights as an employer if one of your employees decides to quit. In this scenario, you will quickly realize how useful it is to have those job descriptions and employee standards written down for your new hire!

DELEGATING MANAGEMENT

As businesses beccome larger, the size and complexity of the enterprise may mean that part or all of the owner's day-to-day management will need to be assigned to other people. Again, just as the owner-operator's role changed when the business grew from an owner-only enterprise to a business with a small team of employees, the owner-manager's role changes as the company reaches each new stage of development. The skills needed to run a business through a team of managers are different than that of running a business through a team of employees.

Another reason you may choose to systematically delegate management is to prepare your business for ownership transition. You may wish to reduce your active day-to-day involvement and pursue other interests, or you may have identified a buyer or successor for your business who you want to transition into management. We will address the subject of ownership transition in more detail in Chapter 7 as part of the discussion about managing risks.

No matter what the reason for your decision to delegate some or all management functions in your business, it remains vital for you to maintain overall leadership, providing guidance at a strategic level. However, you must also give your managers autonomy by delegating responsibility for both the practical aspects of accomplishing various internal processes and accountability for the results they achieve.

As management issues become more complex, it's timely to re-emphasize the role of advisers. This is a wise investment that provides an arm's-length perspective that may help you identify human resources–management strategies that become key success factors.

HUMAN RESOURCES MANAGEMENT DRIVES PRODUCTIVE BUSINESSES

A key reason your customers have chosen to do business with you is your employees. Customer satisfaction is highly correlated with employee satisfaction. Your employees are often the face of your business, so their level of engagement will directly impact your customers, especially in service businesses. Customers will often forget a mistake, but they will remember how your staff dealt with it. Were they indifferent or sincere in their efforts? If a key objective for you is to improve customer satisfaction, one of the first places to start is with your staff.

When we encountered businesses with bright and cheerful employees—those who seemed to exude a can-do attitude, and everyone seemed to be on the same page—it really made us sit back and ask, "What's different here?"

Talking to the owners or managers of these businesses, we realized that often the key seemed to be a real touch for what are loosely referred to as "people skills." Our sense is that these skills get better as people focus on them. This attitude is more than just being pleasant. It involves caring for people in such a way that they become invested in effectively contributing to your business goals. People skills clearly require focus and deliberate strategies that hone in on creating an optimal business environment. These strategies work because, at the end of the day, everyone understands and contributes to the process of achieving the goals of the business.

The power of an effective team on a mission to succeed is an awesome thing to behold, and is completely achievable when systematically managed.

7

MITIGATING RISKS

Redtail Vineyard

Gilbert Provost and Pauline Joicey took their passion for wine and created a fully solar-powered vineyard and winery in Prince Edward County, Ontario. The first vines at Redtail Vineyard were planted in June 2004. Since then, Redtail grapes have produced two quality varieties: Pinot Gris and Pinot Noir.

Redtail is a small winery, producing five hundred to seven hundred cases of its organic offering each year. Gilbert and Pauline plan to remain small. "Other wineries often import grapes from elsewhere to create their wines," says Pauline. "We only produce what we grow."

Changes in wine consumption rates are one risk in their business. "People in France are turning away from wine—consumption is down," says Gilbert. To lessen this risk, they ensure that they are producing a high-quality product that wine connoisseurs will seek out. "If the quality isn't there, the label doesn't go on the bottle," he says. However, the influences of other trends have been helping the wine market, particularly in North America. "Wine has gone a long way from being seen as a sinful product to something with a good health component." Creating an organic product is an added enticement in this market.

Their primary risk factor is the weather. "It's a difficult challenge—we have zero control over it," Pauline says. However, they have worked on a variety of tactics to help lessen this risk. Gilbert has been keeping track of temperatures over the last five years to follow climate patterns in an effort to anticipate what elements could have a negative effect. They also bury some vines in the winter to insulate them during harsh cold spells.

One of the most important ways they alleviate the weather risks is by regularly keeping an eye on the plants—typically every day. "We're not weekend growers," says Gilbert. Mildew is a weather-related problem that happens every year. "It's just what the extent of it is. If you get in early, you have a chance to treat it." In 2006, the mildew problem was exceptionally damaging for many farmers. Some fields were so badly affected that the growers abandoned them. By keeping on top of the issue, Pauline and Gilbert were able to treat the problem, alleviating the risk of having a devastating year. Visit the company's website at **www.redtailvineyard.com**.

By their very nature, successful entrepreneurs are optimistic. Over time they have had to overcome numerous unforeseen challenges and they tend to be confident in their ability to prevail over whatever comes their way. It may be this optimism that puts the discussion of mitigating risk factors far down the list of priorities for some entrepreneurs. Yet there are many risk factors that can quickly limit the growth potential of your business. Risks can derail the best-laid plans.

Risks can be in the form of catastrophic events, such as a fire on the business premises or the death of one of the owners or key employees. Or they can be more systemic in nature, subtly undermining your strategies over time. Consider the risk introduced by a poorly trained employee in a service department, or the lack of a key resource such as labour.

Risks can be further categorized based on the likelihood of them occurring. Catastrophic events can devastate the business in a very short period, but generally have a lower probability of occurring. Other risks may have a higher likelihood of occurring, but may not be disastrous to business; still others may more slowly impact the business. Anticipating the risks to your business and taking steps to mitigate them before they happen will protect your enterprise.

A RISK-MANAGEMENT MODEL

With each of the risks we will discuss, the successful businesses we met took specific steps to manage them. They used a process to identify and manage risks:

1. Identify the source of the risks.
2. Be proactive in anticipating their impact.
3. Take steps to mitigate the risks.
4. Identify strategies to avoid the risks.
5. Adapt quickly when risk levels become unacceptable.

This becomes a model or a repeatable process that can be used to protect your business.

An Example: The Risk of Declining Sales

Without sales, there is no business. Clearly this is a significant risk. However, for businesses that have cultivated a loyal group of repeat customers by delivering high-quality products or services, the risk of losing those customers is significantly less than the business that relies on customers who are chasing the lowest price.

Each business model has its own intrinsic risks. For the business that delivers value by leveraging after-sales service, and expertise, unplanned events could erode the company's reputation or undermine its service quality. Loss of key staff could negatively affect customer service. For the business pursuing low cost as its primary competitive advantage, access to low-cost products or services while maintaining efficient business operations creates another set of risks that could result in declining sales.

Let's consider how we might use the risk-management model to address the risk of declining sales and create a proactive program that sets out a definitive response strategy.

1. Identify the Source of Risk

- Why do your customers buy from you? Is it price, quality, service, expertise, or reputation?
- What factors might negatively influence their decision to buy in the future, based on each of the attributes you have identified?
- Depending on why your customers buy from you, identify

those aspects of your business that are critical to sustaining your ongoing ability to deliver the attributes that give your product or service a competitive advantage. Do your capabilities hinge on certain people, suppliers, processes, locations, or any other factor?

- In a declining market, your strengths will be your primary advantage and become the attributes you must first protect.

2. Be Proactive in Anticipating the Impact of Risk Factors

- With the critical risk factors affecting sales identified, anticipate the degree to which they could impact sales. Focus on those factors with the highest impact and highest likelihood of occurring first.
- You can reduce the impact of either a catastrophic event, or a systemic threat by anticipating what can go wrong.
- Conduct a systematic evaluation of your business from a risk perspective, mapping out the type of risks you are exposed to, and the degree to which they materially affect your sales results.

3. Take Steps to Mitigate the Risk

- Having identified the risk factors that have the highest potential to negatively affect sales, consider how you can protect those elements of your business that sustain your ability to deliver them.
- If it's the loss of an employee that's the risk, are you taking care of him or her with competitive compensation, with

effective rewards, and by creating a positive and rewarding workplace?

- If access to a supplier is critical to allow you to offer a particular product for sale, are you protecting your credit relationship and managing day-to-day interactions with that supplier in a responsible way?

4. Identify Alternatives that Avoid the Risk

- Have you identified alternatives that would give you an option if one of your critical attributes was jeopardized?
- If you are relying on one person for a key function, have you taken steps to train an alternate as backup?
- If you are relying on a single supplier, can you secure exclusivity in your marketplace, or have you cultivated relationships with other suppliers that could be substituted?

5. Adapt Quickly When Risk Levels Become Unacceptable

- Failure to respond is itself a critical risk factor. Be attentive to early indicators of sales problems, and when you see them, address them head on.
- You will have the best results when you act early, whether the risks are matters of consumer preference, competitive challenges, internal process, or service deterioration.
- You will likely be overcome by a risk factor when you simply hope it will go away!

We have applied the risk-management model to the issue of growing sales. This same model can also be applied to any area of your business you think may be vulnerable.

Pilates North

We met twin sisters Rachel and Lisa Schklar in Chapter 3, in which they offered insights into aspects of cash flow in their successful Pilates fitness enterprise.

One of the biggest threats in their business involves losing trainers. While an employee leaving might seem to be a simple human resources issue, in the case of their type of enterprise it's not. "Basically, we can lose clients to trainers," says Rachel. "When the trainer leaves, there's the risk that the clients will follow them." And losing clients obviously affects future sales.

They mitigate this threat by addressing both sides of the equation: the trainers and the customers. First, by creating a great work environment that their employees want to come to each day, they lessen the risk that an employee will want to leave in the first place. Second, by working hard to create a sense of loyalty in their clients and giving them an atmosphere they enjoy, they are more likely to sign up the client to a new set of classes even if a favourite trainer decides to leave.

Identifying Areas of Risk in Your Business

Before defining your plans to mitigate key risks, you need to identify the risks themselves. The best place to start is your business plan.

Consider all the sections and subsections of your business

plan. Review your assumptions and potential threats to your business. For example, your business plan clearly identifies your target customer segment, and its needs, and how you will meet them. Are there risks that will have an impact on your ability to sell to this segment? What about the competition or the industry? Are there certain trends that may have a negative impact on your target segment?

Also consider the financial aspects of your business plan. What key financial assumptions have you made and what is your plan to deal with volatility? For example, do exchange rates impact the cost of your products? What if those exchange rates suddenly change? How will this affect your business? Use hypothetical examples to help you understand the assumptions by plugging them into profit and loss forecasts and cash-flow projections. You can quickly assess the impact on your financial position if, for example, your revenue remains stable and your costs go up 15 per cent. What if certain costs go up more . . . or less?

The business plan provides a framework to consider the risks in your business, to understand their significance, and to begin to identify and assess strategies to mitigate them.

Reducing Business Continuity Threats

There are some dire situations that, by their very nature, pose critical threats to a business: fire, death of an owner or key employees, and legal settlements are just a few. However, because they are situations faced by virtually all businesses, the solutions for each have been provided for either by sharing the risk (in the case of insurance coverage) or with tried-and-true strategies that are well understood—and relatively easy to accomplish. Here's a quick list.

Shared Risk	Tried-and-True Strategy
fire	fire insurance
theft	theft insurance
technology failure	business interruption insurance; disaster recovery plan
public liability	general liability insurance
death of the owner	life insurance, creation and updating of will, and succession planning
death of a key employee	key employee insurance
disability of an owner	disability insurance and power of attorney
death of a business partner	partnership agreement and life insurance on the life of the partner

Contingency Plans

Taking the time to map out the risks that could affect the continuity of their business and create effective contingency plans is a task many small business owners prefer to avoid. After all, there is always tomorrow to think about potential problem areas. Nevertheless, if you need motivation to address contingency planning, look no further than your family, your employees or your clients. Consider how they will also be affected by an interruption—or even a profound failure—in your business. Contingency plans create practical responses to each key business continuity threat listed and answer the question "How would my business survive and thrive if . . . ?"

The wisdom of those business owners who recognize the

benefits of effective contingency planning can be seen in those companies that have made provisions for the resources they will need to weather a catastrophic event. The continuity of these businesses over time—often over generations—and the livelihood they provide to employees are testaments to the importance of continuity planning.

If you have not created contingency plans to deal with your critical business continuity issues, close this book immediately, and do it now! Nothing could be more important.

Atelier Mécanique Alain Careau Inc.

With more than twenty years' experience as a mechanic, Alain Careau opened his car repair business in the Quebec City suburb of L'Ancienne-Lorrette in 2006. Although his specialty is electronic components, he expanded his services to include general car repair because it's a more common need.

Alain is a perfectionist and very hands-on. "I give my customers my personal guarantee at all times. My goal is to keep a customer for life."

Soon after beginning his business, Alain discovered a simple but significant financial risk in his business: not being paid by his clients. "When I started, I learned the hard way that I had to collect from my retail customers immediately rather than later. I lost approximately $8,000 in the first year of business."

Alain put measures in place to prevent this from happening again. "With this experience under my belt, I quickly learned to do one job at a time and get paid before completing another job on the same car. I accept credit cards as well as cash, and customers pay before they leave the shop."

In addition, he provides customers with various options to

ensure the repairs will fit their budget, such as a choice of different-quality parts. "I've also learned to choose my customers. Given the small-town mentality, you learn who pays well and who doesn't."

Reducing Financial Risks

Protecting the financial integrity of your business minimizes the risk of it not having adequate financial resources to achieve its goals. Financial integrity includes a number of considerations, including reliable record keeping, adequacy of cash flow, maintaining access to credit, tax minimization strategies, and estate and succession planning.

Previous chapters have addressed specific aspects of these topics. However, financial management also benefits from the application of a robust risk-management framework

For example, one of the areas of financial risk is cash flow. We talked to business owners who had mitigated that risk by creating and communicating clearly defined policies to deal with any area of their business that involved cash, incurring of expenses, or the authorization of payments. Consider the following:

- Set limits for the amount of cash maintained on site.
- Set policies that define how often you make deposits at your financial institution, who makes them, when, and where.
- Establish authority levels for invoice payments, with larger expenses requiring more senior approval.
- Create a check and audit function to reconcile all payments after they have been made.

- To whatever degree is possible, separate sales and administrative processes to ensure aggressive sales practices are not pursued at the expense of prudent risk-management strategies.
- Establish policies for granting credit to customers, specific terms for any payments required, and clear collection policies including the point at which no further sales are made to a given account.
- Establish policies for ordering inventory and supplies, and create information systems to guide the decisions of whoever is responsible for purchasing.
- Carefully consider all contracts, including obtaining appropriate legal advice, *before* you sign them.

It's difficult to assess all risks, particularly all financial ones. Often, it's useful to have some general strategies to support your financial position during a crisis. For example, a number of the owners we met keep a certain amount of cash in their bank account just in case. Some used a general guideline of having enough money to cover three to six months' worth of expenses, if their revenue should suddenly stop. Similarly, many business owners ensure they have access to credit, typically in the form of a line of credit. This allows them to meet critical expenses, such as payroll, if there is an unforeseen shortage of cash. Establishing these loan facilities before an emergency situation occurs ensures that they are accessible. It's also important to avoid the temptation of eating into that cushion to fund day-to-day expenses.

Risks Introduced by Technology

Businesses rely on technology to produce and sell their products or services. Maintaining that technology, using its capabilities to the benefit of the business, and upgrading it over time is all part of the process of unlocking the growth potential in a business.

Technology also introduces a variety of risks that must be managed. Many of them will be specific to a given technology, so it is difficult to generalize, but there are some basic principles a small business owner can use to reduce technological risk.

- Effective training increases the benefit of any technology while reducing risks from operator error. Some risks are physical in nature, reputational, or relative to business continuity.
- Proper maintenance of technology increases output, reduces breakdowns, and prolongs the life of a given asset. Establish service schedules, quality checks, and emergency procedures.
- Identify backup alternatives that can be employed in the event of a breakdown or interrupted service. Protect computer data by storing it offsite, arrange for alternate systems on a contingency basis, and be sure you have good service and repair support strategy to respond quickly.

UNLOCKING KEY: The process of identifying both catastrophic and systemic risk factors enables you to construct effective policies and backup plans that minimize the potential for those risks to threaten the business.

Get Growing *for business* Online Resource: The Risk-Factor worksheet provides a framework you can use to identify key risk factors in your business. Using the business plan as a tool to assess the specific risks you may face, the worksheets guide the consideration of mitigation strategies (www.getgrowingforbusiness. com/unlocking/risks).

REDUCING THE RISK IN OWNERSHIP TRANSITION

Many of the business owners we met were second-, third-, or fourth-generation owners who had successfully taken over an existing business, taking it to new levels of success not imagined by the original owner. This is often a long-term goal for many business owners: transfer ownership to the next generation or to a new owner and transition into a financially secure retirement. The statistical reality is much different. Most businesses do not survive to the next generation or do not generate a sale price that is high enough to fund the style of retirement the owner expects.

The best way to reduce these risks is to begin planning ownership transfer early (some say that it should begin the day you first open the doors of your business) and take deliberate steps to address a number of key issues that could potentially undermine your long-term goals. An effective plan will:

- increase and protect the value of your business over time;
- ensure that your business is structured in such a way as to

ensure the value you have created is transferable to a new owner (A key risk is that the business is so tied up with you and your personal relationships, that once you leave the business dies.);

- identify a potential new owner (or owners) with the financial capacity to take over the business;

- identify a potential new owner (or owners) with the skills and abilities to succeed in your particular type of business;

- set out a program that moves the new owner into management roles in such a way as to protect the value of the business;

- address legal and tax issues, ultimately structuring a purchase and sale agreement that meets the needs of both the buyer and the seller;

- define the degree (if any) of your involvement after the sales is completed, whether being actively on site on a day-to-day basis or in a consultative role; and

- maximize the dollars you realize from the sale creating cash that becomes available to fund a secure retirement.

Given the complexities of the various phases of ownership transition, a variety of advisers may contribute to building a successful plan. These advisers may include accountants, lawyers, business bankers, personal financial planners, insurance specialists, succession-planning consultants, and family counsellors. While each situation is different, there are a variety of resources that can help you reduce the risks that come with transitioning ownership and achieving financial stability in retirement.

UNLOCKING KEY: Begin planning ownership transition early and consider the right options for your situation.

> Get Growing *for business* Online Resource: The Succession Planning Checklist provides a framework for business owners considering ownership transition issues (www.getgrowingforbusiness.com/unlocking/risks).

The Role of Communication in Risk Management

It might seem simple, but the best risk-management system you can create in your business is good communication. It's not hard to see why.

When management and staff enjoy an environment in which communication is healthy, they work more effectively as a group and more freely exchange information that can help identify risk factors early and find practical solutions. When people understand the implications of their actions and communicate their effect on other related areas of the business, risks reduce and effectiveness increases.

It may be as simple as communicating safety guidelines or identifying the reasons for negative customer trends. There are benefits for everyone when you can create an open, trusting workplace where every team member understands his or her role and works together to contribute to the success of the business.

By making the job of identifying risk factors and developing effective strategies a business-wide goal, you increase your ability to mitigate those factors and find effective alternative mechanisms to protect the continuity of your business.

8

LEADING SUCCESS

Aqua Valley Water Company Ltd.

Daryl Plandowski and Dennis Vial started Aqua Valley Water in Coldbrook, Nova Scotia, in 2005. Using a reverse-osmosis system, they provide purified water to local homes and businesses.

They're not afraid to work—and work hard. "When we started," says Dennis, "we started from scratch! We went knocking on doors for business."

They created a self-serve U-Fill station outside their Coldbrook store to give customers the opportunity to purchase their water during off-hours. "This way water is available 24/7," says Dennis. "Plus, you can view the entire purification process. It's very visual."

The self-serve station was so successful that they opened a U-Fill-only location in nearby New Minas. Their vision is to have twenty-five U-Fills in the next two years. "It's very aggressive," Dennis says.

In the meantime, they continue to be a part of the community, which is very important to them. They donate water to various groups, and also give their time to soccer, hockey, and volunteering.

These business partners are determined, and have been from the get-go. "You need to be hands-on, especially early in the game. We like to keep moving."

This chapter is about leadership. The business owners we met on our cross-Canada tour had a lot to tell us about the process of effectively leading their businesses. They showed us how effective leaders move their businesses forward—toward their vision of future success. From one business owner to the next, we saw different styles of leadership. However, the strongest leaders demonstrated an approach that was forward thinking and action oriented, with an overflowing and infectious level of enthusiasm!

As we begin the final chapter of a book that seeks to provide the keys to unlocking the potential in your small businesses, leadership is the right place to focus our attention. Leadership is the final key that pulls everything together.

The previous chapters covered a lot of ground, looking in detail at:

- establishing personal and business goals;
- the planning process;
- executing effective sales and marketing strategies;
- managing cash flow;
- finding ways to manage costs;
- acquiring financing;

- managing human resources; and
- mitigating risks.

While each aspect is important in and of itself, it was clear to us that a business owner's ability to lead is the glue that holds the whole enterprise together. It's what keeps everything on track.

KEY DIMENSIONS OF LEADERSHIP

There are three primary dimensions to strong leadership, each of which answers one of three fundamental questions about the business: Where are we going? How are we going to get there? Are we delivering?

1. A Vision of the Future: Where Are We Going?

Earlier, we discussed how to establish personal and business goals and then translate them into a mission statement that becomes the focal point for your business, and reflects your vision for the business. Clearly, creating the mission statement is only part of the story. We've all likely seen businesses where that document is tacked to the wall in the lunch room, or above the order desk. But it takes more than just a slogan on the wall to make the sentiment a reality. Effective leadership puts the mission into action—owns it, lives it, and makes it infectious. This type of leadership points the way for the business and defines where it is headed.

We recall one restaurant owner we met who had a clear vision of where she was taking her enterprise. She pictured her storefront as the cornerstone of an exciting, lively, revitalized community where people could live, play, and enjoy the benefits of a multi-faceted urban environment. That vision underscored every conversation we had with her. She took it beyond just words, becoming actively involved in her local business community and working to make her vision into a reality that extended well beyond her enterprise.

For her, the answer to the question, "Where are we going?" clearly guided every aspect of her interaction with her neighbours, her customers, and her staff. It was a part of every decision she had about how she would promote her restaurant (as well as the local community where it was located) and her menu, and it engendered a sense of excitement in everyone with whom she interacted. She was leading many people toward her clear vision of the future.

Business owners with this type of clear vision point out some key leadership priorities:

Customer Focus

Make the process of creating value for your customers central to your leadership. When customers are the focal point for your vision of the future, they will help you anchor your business's competitive advantage. Paying close attention, listening to your customers, and hearing what they are telling you will help you orient your strategies and leadership focus. Ground the vision for your business in the insights you gain from your customers.

Strategic Thinking

Effective leaders are able to identify critical problems, find workable solutions, and translate them into short- and long-term plans that will turn their vision into a reality. Some do this in isolation. Other owners engage broad circles of people to contribute ideas or perspectives. There is no one right way to approach the task, but leaders who fail to devote the necessary effort risk creating a vision of the future that is ineffective as a business model, which ultimately fails the practical tests of the real world.

Strategic Influencing

It's one thing to know where you are going in business, but it's another to convince others to join you—and gain their commitment to the process. Leaders influence staff, customers, business service providers, and key stakeholders. They build consensus, foster buy-in, and move all the people they touch toward their vision of the future.

2. Focus on Action: "How Are We Going to Get There?"

With a clear vision of where the business is going, good leaders begin to take action that will move the business forward. They move beyond the conceptual, positioning themselves and their teams toward actively making things happen.

Communication

Good communication is essential. Engaging everyone who will be carrying out the business plan requires an effective and open dialogue. Leadership fosters communication that is clear, candid, and respectful in all situations. Effective leaders create an environment where information is effectively exchanged and people are free to discuss their own ideas.

Building Team and Personal Capabilities
Leaders inspire and facilitate strong performance. They enable others' skills, developing and directing the momentum of the team toward a common goal.

Building Strong Business Networks
When it comes time to take action, leaders who have a strong network from which to draw ideas, resources, advice, and relevant perspective are much better equipped to succeed and sustain action than those who work in isolation.

3. Focus on Execution: "Are We Delivering?"
Executing the business plan and monitoring its effectiveness is the third area in which leadership skills make a significant difference in the business's results. Some people are skilled in general management—clearly an important skill that creates a level of oversight and direction for all the processes within a business. But not all general managers are leaders. There is a difference between managerial oversight and leadership. Leadership facilitates change, focuses on results, models a sense of pride, and celebrates the successes of others.

Managing Change
There is a constant process of adaptation that must happen whenever a system, product, or service changes. Leaders are aware of this and ensure the business will not only overcome the associated risks with implementing change, but also benefit from the advantages they can deliver. Leaders help people cope with change—which is a common challenge—and ensure that the changes that do occur are desirable, and contribute to overall effectiveness.

Results Focused

Leaders keep their eye on the goal, ensure that the details within a business are attended to, and inspire others to do the same. Daily results must achieve the business's original goals, and processes should continually improve. When results do not meet expectations, leaders respond immediately, consistently evaluating the effectiveness of business plans, strategies, and tactics.

Rewarding Success

Building effective rewards and recognition into the business's operational framework helps recognize staff contributions. The business can distinguish itself in a competitive marketplace only if everyone achieves high standards. Effective leaders seek out opportunities to create an environment that celebrates personal excellence and business successes.

BUILDING YOUR PERSONAL LEADERSHIP INVENTORY

We have met small business owners who seemed to have that innate charisma that we often associate with strong leaders. They have a natural enthusiasm and the ability to motivate others, and they may very well have simply been born with it. But we also met effective leaders who had to make a point of deliberately focusing on building their leadership skills. They regularly assessed their own leadership style, seeking to understand their strengths and to find ways to develop those skills that needed improvement.

It's probably fair to say that whether you're born with

leadership skills or must focus on developing them, leadership is always a journey as opposed to a destination. And journeys don't just happen—there is work to be done along the way.

UNLOCKING KEY: Effective leaders regularly evaluate their personal leadership skills, seeking awareness of their own strengths and weaknesses while actively creating opportunities to increase their effectiveness through training, practice, and experience.

Get Growing *for business* Online Resources: The Leadership Skills Inventory worksheet helps you assess your own leadership competencies (**www.getgrowing-forbusiness.com/unlocking/leadership**).

IN SEARCH OF THE PERFECT LEADER

After considering the vision, action, and delivery dimensions of leadership, and having done your own inventory of personal leadership skills, you may be left feeling a bit overwhelmed.

Let's be clear. After speaking with hundreds of business owners, we did not discover a magic combination of skills and abilities that created a perfect leader. We can report that there appears to be no magic formula that can deliver leadership in a bottle. We did meet people who knew their own capabilities, were deliberate about using their own strengths, and were attentive to opportunities to improve their leadership skills.

There are also a wide variety of business environments which call for different leadership skills. For some, leadership meant keeping themselves moving forward in a part-time enterprise where they were the only employee. For others, their businesses were more complex, with elaborate processes and larger teams, resulting in a different set of leadership demands. One set of leadership skills might be perfect for an agricultural enterprise, but not for a retail operation.

Talking to other business owners in a similar enterprise or industry is a good way to determine what skills will be the most important for you. You can also do a little research to see if there is a related association that caters to the needs of a particular type of business, and seek out the expertise it might offer.

What happens when you're just not cut out for one aspect of leadership or another? Some business owners look for ways to augment their skills by finding people who can provide the missing elements, then delegating some of the leadership responsibilities to them.

In some cases it meant bringing in a partner who was good at managing the day-to-day operations of the business. (Some businesses were fortunate to start with partners who had complementary skills.) In other cases, it meant hiring experts to deal with communication and performance issues. Yet others focused on training to increase the effectiveness of employees who were ready to assume new leadership responsibilities, or alternately to increase their own leadership skills. Whatever your approach, the process is the same:

1. Understand the key dimensions of leadership you need in your business.

2. Do a self-assessment of your skills and abilities.
3. Make a choice to augment your skills through the skills of others, or begin a process of training and development to enhance your own abilities.

Ingrained Style Furniture Company

We met Mike and Alisen Dopf in Chapter 3, where we learned about the steps they've taken to improve cash flow in their custom furniture business, Ingrained Style.

The husband and wife team are committed to the company's mission: to provide excellent quality, fine furniture at a reasonable price, while allowing customers to individualize their piece by choosing the stain and finishing style.

Their partnership is enhanced by the fact that they both bring different skills to the table. "We are complementary in our strengths," says Alisen. "Mike does the sales and product creation, as well as the custom designs. I do the finances, marketing, and communications." Together they provide strong leadership by uniting their skills, and effectively addressing the broad range of skills needed to run a thriving business.

LEADERS MAKE DECISIONS

Ultimately, even though they may take input from a variety of different sources, small business owners make the final decisions for their businesses. These decisions chart the course the business will follow. Effective leaders understand the implications of the decisions they make and how they make them.

How do you make decisions? Are you the type of leader who waits to make a decision until you gather all the relevant facts, consult with internal and external experts, test your ideas with advisers or customers, then systematically weigh the advantages or disadvantages of one approach over another? Or do you pull from your experience, and "go with your gut"?

How long does it take you to make a decision? Do you delay doing so because you want to investigate just one more thing? Leaders take many approaches to decision making.

As a leader you will be called on to make some urgent decisions; however, other issues will operate on a longer timeline. The key is to make sure you know the difference between the two. Some opportunities present themselves for only a short period of time, and while it might be ideal to have more time to gather more information, you will have to make a decision with what you have. Or, conversely, when an opportunity presents itself you may jump at it too quickly, failing to factor in critical elements of the situation that would become evident only after careful analysis and consideration.

As a leader you can take steps to help you make effective decisions.

- Stay informed about general issues that provide a good context for decisions you need to make relative to your business. Read up on current information and gather relevant perspectives.
- Cultivate a group of advisers whom you can call on to help you make key decisions. Incorporate people with specific expertise (peers in your industry, financial and legal advisers, and risk-management resources) and seek out their input when making related decisions.

- Avoid procrastination when faced with a decision. Understand your own strengths and weaknesses relative to making timely, informed decisions. Hold yourself accountable by setting and achieving acceptable standards of timeliness. Consider enlisting the help of others to hold you accountable for meeting deadlines. Procrastination can actually be a negative form of decision making: you are essentially deciding to be inactive!

- Realize that not every decision you make will be the right one. While you can increase your success rate by incorporating others' input, ultimately you will sometimes make the wrong choice. Effective leaders do not get so invested in their own decisions that they are unable to see when something has gone wrong. Be willing to be wrong, and use the information you gain through your mistakes to make better decisions the second time around. (And by the way, the second decision may still be wrong, but use the same "willingness to be wrong" to inform the third decision . . . and so on.)

GET GROWING

If you own a business, you know first-hand that small business owners manage an astonishing number of issues at any given time. You've probably been adding your personal examples to those we've discussed as you've read through these pages. There is a lot for a small business owner to manage. Leadership can get complicated!

And yet, for the most part, the business leaders we met spoke of the opportunities they see in their businesses as opposed to all of the challenges they struggle with. They point to the potential first. The story we heard almost every time was about what these business owners are creating and the things they are accomplishing in their enterprises. Theirs was a message of optimism even during difficult times.

We've said that leading business success is more about the journey than the destination. Having read this book, we trust that the people we have introduced you to, and the lessons we've learned from them, will help you as you continue your journey toward accomplishing your business goals.

Our cross-country journey reminded us that while small businesses may operate in isolated enterprises, there is no need for them to be alone in their endeavours. We were constantly reminded that many businesses deal with exactly the same issues. Where one has found a solution to a particular challenge or a way to capitalize on an opportunity, we saw a willingness to share those perspectives for the benefit of others. It is our hope that the advice and information we have passed along from these businesses to you has helped facilitate that exchange of ideas.

If you have linked to any of the Get Growing *for business* online resources mentioned throughout this book, you've probably already met some of the business owners who are taking the conversation further by joining the discussion forums on the website. It's another opportunity to dig deeper into the collective wisdom of small business owners and to continue to build on your ability to grow your small business success.

If you haven't joined the online discussion, we want to extend our invitation to you directly. Log on to **getgrowingforbusiness.com/unlocking**. Join the conversation. Benefit from access to tools and resources designed to help you unlock the potential in your small business! It's been an exciting cross-country tour of discovery for us, and we know the conversation can be a journey of discovery for you, too.

ADVICE FROM ACROSS CANADA

We leave the last word to some of the entrepreneurs we spoke with from coast to coast. Here is but a sample of their wisdom, advice, and enthusiasm. They've made the decision to get growing, and are unlocking the potential in their small business every day.

"Dare to do! Dare to dream! And dream big!"
—Jeannette Arsenault, Cavendish Figurines Ltd.

"Have a plan before you jump in. Do research on what you're getting into."
—Pauline Joicey, Redtail Vineyard

"Be patient when you're starting off. In year one, you think, 'It's gotta be better than this.' It's easy to bail out after a year and a half. Have determination."
—Dennis Vial, Aqua Valley Water Company

"It's all about the customer. Make them happy and deliver an experience to them—you'll prosper."
—Doug Milburn, Protocase

"If you get complacent, be ready to close your doors. Strive to be better every day."
—Jeff Roberts, Center City Tire & Auto

"Stay out of debt. Once you're overextended, it puts you in a difficult position."
—Alisen Dopf, Ingrained Style Furniture Company

"Try to work in an area that you're passionate about."
—Cathy Siskind-Kelly, Black Fly Beverage Company Inc.

"Go for it! It's not enough to just live the dream; you have to realize it to see it through."
—Davin Peterson, Base Technology Ltd.

"Consider the dream of starting a small business. You get the reward of being in charge and you own your days."
—Kiera Newman, KIVA Design Build Inc.

"Persistence, persistence, persistence! I feel that it takes about ten years to establish any business. During that time persistence is one character trait that is invaluable."
—Aniko Dunford, EnviroSeal Engineering Products Ltd.

"Offer the best that you have, deliver more than the customer is expecting, and follow up."
—Donna Murphy, Shin Wa Kan Dojo

"Do what is best for your customers. Understand their needs, make sure you provide them with options, and think long term. Your customers will always come back if you provide them with the appropriate advice, even though you might not make the initial sale."
—Alain Careau, Atelier Mécanique Alain Careau Inc.

"Know your market. Do your research before starting your business. And find the lender that will help you out."
—Jeff Gunn, Stonehame Lodge & Chalets

ACKNOWLEDGEMENTS

It's taken a huge group of amazing people to bring this book together. We'd like to thank the hundreds of business owners we met across Canada in the summer of 2008 and those we've reconnected with recently. Thanks to the business owners who shared their stories, and special thanks to those who gave us permission to include them in this book: Jeannette Arsenault and Don Maxfield (Cavendish Figurines Ltd.), Derek Barr (Chocolate Barr's Candies Inc.), Alain Careau (Atelier Mécanique Alain Careau Inc.), Yola and Forbes Christie (Windward Flutes), Mike and Alisen Dopf (Ingrained Style Furniture Company), Aniko Dunford (EnviroSeal Engineering Products Ltd.), Perry Floreani and Annette Remboulis (Innovation Image Inc.), Doug Glancy and Kiera Newman (KIVA Design Build Inc.), Jeff and Don Gunn (Stonehame Lodge and Chalets), Murray Hannigan (Hannigan Honey Inc.),

Rob Kelly and Cathy Siskind-Kelly (Black Fly Beverage Company Inc.), Steve Lilley and Doug Milburn (Protocase), Donna Murphy (Shin Wa Kan Dojo), Jeffrey Norman (J&L PowerSports Unlimited), Russ Pelley (GRI Simulations Inc.), Davin Peterson (Base Technology Ltd.), Gilbert Provost and Pauline Joicey (Redtail Vineyard), Jeff Roberts (Center City Tire & Auto), Rachel and Lisa Schklar (Pilates North), and Dennis Vial and Daryl Plandowski (Aqua Valley Water Ltd.). Their collective wisdom and willingness to make those insights available to other small business owners made this book possible.

Our journey across the country took us away from home for long periods of time: a special thank you to our wives and families for their strong support throughout.

The tour and this book were a team effort in so many ways. The small business advisers who work in our branches across the country helped by introducing us to these special customers. Our home team (a.k.a. the Toronto group here on the tenth floor) supported us while we were on the road, with marketing and agency teams keeping us on track. Our advance public relations group, Deborah Clark, Patty Stathokostas, and the rest of their team helped co-ordinate the dozens of media reports and tracked our progress. And let's not forget our trusty driver Andrew Felice, who criss-crossed the country not once but twice as he skillfully delivered us on time and in one piece.

Thank you, Samantha Mesrobian, Anna Simmons, and Key Porter Books editors Carol Harrison and Linda Pruessen, for your work in fine-tuning the stories captured in this book, helping to pull it all together with patient rewrites, editing, and outstanding professionalism throughout.

INDEX